PARENTING WHEN SEPARATED
Helping Your Children Cope and Thrive

Dr John Sharry is a mental health professional with over twenty-five years' experience, a bestselling author of ten positive psychology and parenting books, developer of the award-winning Parents Plus Programmes and a weekly health columnist for the *Irish Times*. His books have been translated into nine languages including Spanish, Japanese, Chinese and Arabic. See www.solutiontalk.ie and www.parentsplus.ie for more details.

Dubli·
Baile Átha

—

D0928366

Parenting when Separated

Helping Your Children
Cope and Thrive

John Sharry

VERITAS

Published 2014 by
Veritas Publications
7–8 Lower Abbey Street
Dublin 1
Ireland
publications@veritas.ie
www.veritas.ie

ISBN 978 1 84730 573 2

10 9 8 7 6 5 4 3 2 1

Designed by Barbara Croatto, Veritas Publications
Printed in Ireland by Castle Print Ltd, Galway

Veritas books are printed on paper made from the wood pulp of managed
forests. For every tree felled, at least one tree is planted, thereby renewing
natural resources.

This book is dedicated to the hundreds of parents I have had the privilege of working with over the last twenty-five years, who, despite adversity and challenge, have remained resourceful and hopeful parents for their children. The inspiration for the ideas in this book comes directly from their experience and wisdom.

ACKNOWLEDGEMENTS

In writing the book, I would like to acknowledge the contribution of Michelle Murphy and Adele Keating with whom I co-developed the Parents Plus – Parenting When Separated Programme, and also of Eugene Donohoe and Peter Reid with whom I wrote previous books on this subject.

I would also like to thank all my colleagues in the Parents Plus Charity and the Mater Child and Adolescent Mental Health Service where I worked for sixteen years. I'm also grateful to the *Irish Times,* particularly the Health Plus editors, Deridre Veldon, John Collins and Joyce Hickey, for the opportunity to write on the subject of family life each week and for giving permission for many of my columns to be published in this book.

Contents

INTRODUCTION

Separation and divorce are on the increase. More and more children are witnessing their parents separate and/or growing up in single-parent households. The chain of events from parental conflict to separation and divorce can have a devastating impact on parents, children and extended families. In surveys, parental separation is second only to the death of a parent in the levels of stress it can cause in children and parents. In addition, separation can bring many other stressful events to bear, such as house moves, money problems, legal battles and loss of supportive relationships, all of which can increase the burden on parents and children.

The Purpose of this Book

The purpose of this book is to help parents help themselves and their children to cope better with separation and divorce. The book includes practical advice and suggestions that are based on extensive research into what makes a difference for children coming to terms with their parents' separation.

The Good News

The good news is that there are positive things you can do that will minimise the negative impact of separation on your children. According to research studies, children can suffer a range of emotional and social difficulties on account of their parents' separation. A significant number of children cope relatively well, however, and this book will help to point you in that direction.

Their coping positively largely depends on how their parents manage the separation. To achieve this, it is essential that as parents you make some headway towards achieving the following goals.

» Take steps to manage your own stress to ensure you personally are coping.
» Listen to your children and focus on their best interests and needs.
» Work constructively with your former partner on parenting issues.
» Maintain the quality of your own parenting.
» Minimise the changes in your child's life after the separation.

If you can do these things, then you are doing a lot to help your children manage the separation, and you are taking steps towards a more harmonious living environment. This book aims to build on what you are already doing right and to further improve your own and your children's coping.

Achieving Shared Parenting

Throughout this book, the importance of achieving shared parenting after the separation is emphasised. Though there are exceptions (e.g. in cases of violence or abuse), shared parenting is generally the best situation for most children post-separation. Shared parenting gives children access to the care, support and love of their two parents, working together for the benefit of their children. These are the ideal conditions in which children can thrive and grow up as well-adjusted adults.

It is acknowledged, however, that this ideal is far from easy; in reality, many parents find themselves either as single parents coping relatively on their own with their children, or as 'live-away' parents struggling to stay supportively involved in their children's lives. Though the situation is changing (as more fathers have an active role in childcare before and after separation), the ideal of shared parenting is still relatively rare. The most common situation is for the children to live with one parent (usually the mother) and then have weekly or less frequent access with the other parent (usually the father). For this reason, two chapters are included that focus on the respective experiences and challenges of being a single and a live-away parent. As a parent reading these chapters you may find yourself identifying with either or both perspectives. Indeed the roles are often interchangeable, and you may have the dual experience of being both a single parent when the children are with you and of being a live-away parent when they are with your former partner.

Also recognised is the importance of step-parents and new partners in blended families, not to mention grandparents and extended family, all of whom play an important role in helping separated parents and supporting their children. Each family is unique and the key is to identify your family strengths and what works for you.

PART 1
Helping Your Children Cope

THE EFFECT OF SEPARATING ON PARENTS

Parental conflict leading to separation and/or divorce is hugely stressful for parents. The turmoil and devastation can last a long time. It can be a long, arduous journey lasting many years, starting with the awareness of difficulties in your relationship to the final decision to separate and then on to the path of developing stable separate living arrangements for you and your children.

Before the decision to separate there may be a long period of uncertainty and upset, of breaks and reconciliations, and often very open conflict. After the separation there can be a long period of instability as lifestyles and living arrangements are thrown into turmoil. It is not surprising that during this period you may feel you are really in for a rough ride. You can feel depressed, deeply hurt, guilty, angry, outraged, even suicidal and homicidal. You may feel your whole world has caved in, that your dreams are shattered, that you are a failure because you haven't made your relationship or marriage work.

You can also be acutely aware of the distress of your children and be plagued by guilt about this. In addition, there can be great stigma and shame associated with being separated. Whereas with a terrible event like bereavement you can be guaranteed the support of your family and friends, sometimes there is less support when you have separated. People are often looking for whose fault it is and someone to blame and this can add to the burden.

When parents separate, they are usually at very different stages in the process. Rarely do both parties arrive at the decision at the same time. One parent is usually unhappy and upset in the relationship or marriage for a long time and then initiates the separation. This parent can go through great upset and guilt at ending the relationship and because of the hurt caused to the children and their former partner. The other parent is liable to feel shock and devastation. They can feel deeply hurt, guilty and wounded as they come to terms with the fact that the relationship is finally over. Though parents start out at different stages, over time they tend to move through the whole range of feelings. Whether they initiated the separation or not, both parents can swing between feeling hurt and victimised by the other to feeling very guilty at causing the relationship or marriage to end.

As well as the negative feelings associated with parental separation, there can also be feelings of relief and new hope. This is especially the case if the relationship has been conflictual and unhappy for some time or indeed if it has been abusive. The separation can be the end of a long process and signify an opportunity for parents to begin to put their difficulties behind them and to start life again.

Whatever point you are at in the separation process, be prepared for a rollercoaster of emotions and a difficult and challenging time for yourself and your children. The best place to start is where you are right now.

Learning to Cope as a Parent

Though it takes time, courage and great compassion, parents do cope with separation and divorce. Some parents may get stuck in resentment, ongoing conflict and disputes, but many parents find the resources to move on, work out a constructive relationship with their former partner, and rebuild their lives for themselves and their children. For your children's sake it is absolutely essential that you do take steps to cope as soon as possible. Whatever their ages, children can suffer greatly on account of their parents' separation. This is especially the case when there is ongoing conflict and bitterness and/or when parents are caught up in their own preoccupations and unable to attend to their children's needs. Children can suffer greatly during parental conflict, separation and divorce and need the support and care of both their parents more than ever.

This can be hard to do if you are weakened and drained emotionally and mentally by your own experience of the separation. Your children, however, need you during this period. Even though you feel at your weakest, you are called on to be at your strongest. Remember you are your child's greatest asset during this difficult time. For this reason you need to take steps to care for yourself and to cope personally, not only for yourself but also for the sake of your children.

So what can you do to help yourself cope during this difficult time?

» TAKE CARE OF YOURSELF AND ENSURE YOU GET SUPPORT: Don't go through this period alone. Make sure you meet and talk to people who you feel can understand and support you. Find friends and family members who can support you emotionally. Remember that extended family members such as grandparents, or close friends, may have their own grief about the end of your relationship or may have a biased view and may not be able to fully support you. If this is the case, try and find people who have some distance from the situation and who can give you a more balanced view. This might mean making contact with old friends and asking for the support you need. If it's helpful, seek out support groups or meetings for separating and separated parents. There are also many counselling services, both general and specific to separating parents, that could be invaluable to you. You will find a list of services at the end of this book.

» GIVE YOURSELF TIME: Remember that coping with separation is a long process and can be cyclical. There will be bad times when you feel low or upset, but remember that these will pass and things will get easier in the long term. Try and maintain an optimistic outlook, focusing on the practical things you can do rather than worrying excessively.

» PRACTISE SELF-CARE AND RELAXATION: Parents under stress often stop eating well or exercising or doing things they enjoy. This can cause even greater stress. This is the time when you really do need to look after yourself, by ensuring you eat well, exercise, get good rest and relaxation and maintain some enjoyable outlets. The more energised and refreshed you can be, the more available you can be for your children.

» BEGIN THE HEALING PROCESS: All things being equal, the hardest thing for parents can be to forgive themselves or their former partner for what has happened and to let go of excessive resentment, hurt and guilt. These strong negative emotions, however, can be damaging. Resentment about your former partner can limit your ability to co-parent and can be indirectly communicated to your children, making it 'not okay' for them to love their other parent. Excessive guilt can cause you to cut off from your children and to have little contact, or if you do have contact, you can overcompensate with permissive parenting. These responses are not helpful to children and are motivated by strong negative emotions. It is important to start the healing process for yourself. The sooner you can accept what has happened, the sooner you can let go of bitterness, resentment and guilt, and the sooner you can be there for your children to help them cope.

HELPING CHILDREN COPE

For children, the conflict leading up to their parents' separation, the separation itself, and coming to terms with new living arrangements are all hugely stressful events. How they cope varies greatly according to their unique temperament, personality and individual needs. Each child is different. It is important that you listen carefully to them so that you can understand how they are coping before you decide how best to help them. One very important factor determining children's coping is their age at the time their parents separate. Below are some guidelines as to how children of different ages experience their parents' separation and what you can do to help.

Pre-schoolers (0–4)

Pre-school children are generally upset and confused by their parents' separation. They find it hard to understand why it is happening and often experience it as a devastating blow to their sense of security. They often worry that if mum and dad have stopped loving each other, then they have stopped loving them too, or they fear that if one parent has left the home, then the other is likely to leave and abandon them also. They often fantasise that they are in some way responsible for the separation, thinking, for example, that mum and dad have split up because they were bold. Pre-schoolers often demonstrate a lot of distressed behaviour, such as night fears, being over-clingy, tantrums and disobedience. They do not have the words to describe how they feel and may instead 'act out' that distress in their behaviour.

HOW TO HELP

Pre-school children need frequent reassurance that mum and dad both still love them, that they did nothing wrong to cause mum and dad to split up, and that they will be taken care of. These reassurances need to be frequent and in a simple language that children can easily understand. It is also very important that any changes of routine and living arrangements are explained clearly to pre-schoolers, preferably in advance and by both parents. Just because pre-schoolers are younger, parents should not argue or criticise each other in front of them, assuming they don't understand what is being said. Even infants pick up on tensions and rows between parents and are adversely affected by them.

A good way to support pre-schoolers after separation is to make sure you spend one-to-one time with them, when you can listen to them, reassure them and play with them. Don't compensate with gifts or toys. What your children need most is your time, love and attention. In addition, young children need frequent contact with the parent who leaves. A gap of a week or two weeks is often far too long and can lead to huge anxiety. Pre-schoolers need frequent regular contact (especially in the immediate days after the separation) to reassure them that mum or dad still loves them and is there for them.

School-age children (5–10)

School-age children generally express a lot of grief, anger and sadness when their parents separate. They generally miss greatly the parent who has left the home (even if they had a poor relationship when he/she was there) and can express a lot of anger about this, sometimes taking it out on the parent who is left at home and caring for them. Though they are more able to understand the reasons for the separation, like younger children they can feel responsible and may fantasise and plan how they can get their parents back together again. They may think that if they behave very well, or indeed very badly, that they may somehow bring mum and dad back together.

Many of these children will hide their feelings (for example, saying they don't mind their parents separating, when in fact they feel terribly rejected and miss greatly the parent who has left) and appear to be coping initially, only to have lots of problems at later dates. Also, when there is serious conflict, some children will take sides, becoming an ally to the custodial parent against the parent who has left, and judging the separation in black and white terms. Often this is due to the children being sensitive to the custodial parent's anger towards the other parent, and their fear that they will be abandoned if they don't agree and toe the line.

HOW TO HELP

School-age children need honest and open communication from their parents about the separation. If there is no hope of a reconciliation this needs to be expressed clearly to them, while at the same time understanding their wish for a reunion. It is important that they are given space to express their feelings, especially their anger and upset. It is really helpful if, as parents (custodial or non-custodial), you can listen to and take on board the upset and the complaints they have about you. Be very sensitive to children who appear to be unaffected by the separation. Make sure they still get special time and attention.

While you can acknowledge that mum and dad may disagree about some things, you should state clearly and repeatedly that you are both still parents to them and emphasise what you still agree about. It is important to work hard to get agreement with the other parent (see next chapter), because this, above all, helps the children to settle. At all costs, avoid putting children in the position where they have to take sides. Give them permission to love the other parent, for example by encouraging them to write, call or send cards. Be open to hearing your children talk positively about the other parent, without feeling resentment or jealousy. It really helps if you too can talk positively to them about the other parent.

As with younger children, it is very helpful to set aside special one-to-one time with your children on a regular or daily basis, when you can provide them with lots of positive attention by playing with them, listening to them and being reassuring as appropriate.

Young Adolescents (11+)

By adolescence, many youngsters are beginning to acquire the ability to think in a much more complicated way. They can now see not only what life is but also what it could or should be. They are also moving towards greater independence from the family, and their peer group becomes very important as a reference point. While this increased independence and better intellectual and social resources can in some ways help adolescents cope with their parents' separation, it can also make things worse for them.

After separation, many adolescents can lose quality contact with one of their parents and this can lead to extra problems. Adolescence can be challenging at the best of times, but without the support of two involved parents these challenges can be greatly increased. Adolescents can feel very angry and upset at their parents' separation. They can cut off from their family, seeking the support of peers instead, and this can lead to anti-social behaviour if the peer group is unsuitable. In addition, teenagers can feel pressure to take sides in parental conflict, and are even faced with choosing which parent they want to live with. Sometimes distraught parents can overdepend on their adolescents emotionally. This can be a burden, making a teenager feel great guilt and worry. Being older, the needs of teenagers very often get missed out during separation.

HOW TO HELP

Separated parents need to communicate honestly and openly with adolescents. Generally, teenagers value being told in an adult way why and how the separation has happened. Remember that teenagers can appreciate that there are two sides to the story and it can be very helpful to explain to them your views and feelings and then to objectively and fairly describe the other parent's views as well. This can relieve them of the burden of having to take sides and help them maintain a connection with both parents.

It is also crucial that parents work hard at connecting with and maintaining their relationship with their adolescents. Don't just assume they are okay; go out of your way to spend time with them and to talk and listen to them. It can be helpful if you can maintain a shared, enjoyable activity that you can do regularly with them (such as going to football, or shopping). Equally, parents need to supervise their teenagers in separated families every bit as much as in intact families. You do your teenagers no favours by being over-relaxed about rules or not taking normal precautions regarding safety (for example, knowing where they are).

Finally, avoid relying emotionally on your teenagers. As a separating parent you do need support and you need to seek this out (see Chapter 2). It is not, however, fair to expect youngsters to provide emotional support to either parent or for them to take on the parenting role with younger children. Equally, make sure your teenagers have access to their own supports outside the family. Don't just leave it up to their peer group. If your teenager is upset, as well as providing support yourself, you could ask an extended family member or a trusted family friend who is popular with your teenager to adopt a supportive role.

Helping Children Cope – Some General Principles

BREAKING THE NEWS OF THE SEPARATION

Dealing with the actual separation and how to break the news to children can be one of the most difficult times for families. Below are some general guidelines. The emphasis and detail needs to be tailored to the particular child and his or her age and development. In general, it seems best to tell the children about the separation, but not until you are certain that the decision is final.

» Try to tell the children together and take time to plan what you are going to say.

» Choose a time when you can be with the children after breaking the news.

» Outline the main arrangements for their schooling, where and with whom they will live, where the other parent will live, and arrangements for ongoing contact with both parents and the extended family.

» Give a clear message that the separation is in no way the fault of the children and that there was nothing they could or should have done to prevent it.

» Emphasise that although you, the parents, are separating, you will still be their parents. The conflict is between the parents, not between the parents and the children.

» Tell the children that both parents love them and that they will always be part of their lives.

» Check if the children have questions and be prepared to answer the same questions again over the next days, weeks and months.

» The children will need to manage the process of telling others, for example, friends at school. Parents should help them think through how they want to do this, and should give a clear message that it is not a secret or something of which the children should be ashamed.

GIVE THE CHILDREN TIME AND SPACE TO EXPRESS THEIR THOUGHTS AND FEELINGS

Children will be upset, need reassurance and the opportunity to talk things through. It is normal and appropriate for children from separated families to feel sad and angry at times about the situation. While it may be hard to listen to, denying children their negative feelings does not help. If you choose a time when you feel calm, then you will be able to let the children talk through their feelings without fearing that you will get angry, upset or critical. Children may need to repeat the same questions about the separation, although you feel you provided good answers the first time. Similarly, as they grow older and can understand more complex matters, they may want to ask different questions. It is best to see their questioning as a process. It may continue over a protracted period. An explanation at the time of the separation is unlikely to be sufficient in the longer term. It is as well to remember that if you feel unable to respond to questioning, then maybe there is another adult around who can do so until you feel ready. Ideally, both parents should be emotionally and physically available to talk openly and honestly to the children.

MINIMISE THE LIFE CHANGES YOUR CHILD HAS TO ENDURE

When parents separate, much of the trauma children suffer is not directly due to the separation itself, but rather on account of the life changes that often occur. Children may experience disruptive changes such as living in a different house, moving far away to a new area, changing schools, or losing contact with friends and extended family members, etc. It is important that these changes be minimised. You may think that moving to a new city will be a fresh start for you and your 'new' family, but you may serve your children better by keeping things stable in their lives, at least for the first few years after the separation. If some changes are inevitable (and they often are), try and maintain other sources of stability in your children's lives. For example, you may have to move house, but your children could stay in the same school, though they may have to travel a little further to get there.

MAINTAIN THE QUALITY OF YOUR PARENTING
In the difficult times of separation, and without the support of a partner, it is easy for parents to let the quality of their parenting slip. Your children, however, need consistent and loving parenting more than ever during this time. They need your encouragement, love and attention as well as your rules, guidance and boundaries, as much if not more than before. Below are some ideas on positive parenting that you can apply in your family.

- » Try and spend individual time with each of your children, when you can play with them, relax and enjoy each other's company.
- » Spend family time together weekly, using the time to plan, discuss rules and chores, and to have fun.
- » Set clear rules with your children and enforce them calmly by using consequences to help them learn to take responsibility (e.g. if your child does not come in on time, then he doesn't go out the next day).
- » Be consistent in your routines and reliable in any promises or arrangements you make. This is especially critical for children who need to rebuild their sense of security.

For more ideas on positive parenting, please see the books *Positive Parenting: Bringing up Responsible, Well-Behaved and Happy Children* and *Parenting Teenagers: A Guide to Solving Problems, Building Relationships and Creating Harmony in the Family*, listed at the end of this book.

ACCEPT THE OTHER PARENT'S ROLE IN YOUR CHILD'S LIFE
Though your former partner may not be an important person in your own life anymore, he/she is likely to be a very important person in your

child's life. Being a good parent means accepting the other parent's role in your child's life and taking steps to support their involvement. See their involvement as an advantage. It is good for children to have two different adults (though living apart) caring for them and involved in their lives. It can also be an advantage for you in helping you share the many responsibilities of bringing up a child. See your child's time with the other parent not as an intrusion, but as a benefit to your child and a 'break' for you.

DON'T CRITICISE THE OTHER PARENT IN FRONT OF THE CHILDREN
While you may feel very negatively about your former partner, it is very distressing for the children to hear frequent criticism of someone that they almost certainly still love and probably greatly miss. Save expressions of frustration and negative feelings for when you talk to other adults who are supporting you and try to speak positively (or at least neutrally) about the other parent in front of your children. It is crucial that you don't compete with your former partner for your children's love, and that you don't put your children in a position where they feel they have to take sides. Forcing your children to take sides is damaging to them. Above all, your children need to know that it is all right for them to love both of you.

DON'T USE YOUR CHILDREN AS 'GO-BETWEENS'
Children in separated families, especially when parents are still very angry with each other, should not be used as 'go-betweens' between adults or as 'spies' on the former partner. While you may feel your former partner is behaving in a totally unreasonable manner, it is not in any way your children's responsibility to serve as a line of communication between you and your former partner. Children placed in this position find it very difficult and report that it is very distressing for them. You are the parents, it is up to you to find a way of dealing with practical adult decisions (see the next chapter on negotiating conflict). Similarly, it is very unhelpful to ask your children to 'spy' on your former partner. If the relationship between the adults is over then each should be free to get on with a new life.

A Final Point

In this chapter we have concentrated on helping children cope with the negative effects of their parents' separation. Research suggests, however, that it is excessive conflict between parents, whether they are living together or not, which seems to have the most damaging effect on children. Indeed, some children may actually blossom post-separation if this means they are relieved from the stresses of living with two parents in conflict, and they can go on to live in a less neglectful, less abusive and more harmonious family environment. Of course, this is not to underestimate the often very considerable stress caused by separation and divorce that many children and their families feel.

In the next chapter we look at what you can do to reduce and manage the conflict between you and the other parent, so as to best serve the interests of your children.

CO-PARENTING/NEGOTIATING
WITH THE OTHER PARENT

If you didn't have children together, separating from your partner would be easier. You could move away, put your past relationship behind you and get on with the rest of your life with little or no contact with your ex. Having children, however, changes everything. Generally, children need the support and involvement of both their parents, which means that not only will you have ongoing contact with your former partner, but also that you have a responsibility to develop a working co-parenting relationship with them. Though this can be very difficult, this is perhaps the single most important thing you can do for your children to help them cope with the separation of their parents. Excessive conflict and ongoing disputes between parents after separation is devastating to children. They easily get caught up in the middle and their relationship with both parents is damaged. Be wary of trying to win one over on your former partner or aiming to gain victory by going to court. The adversarial nature of the court system can increase conflict and bitterness, which can endure far beyond the time a judge has imposed a settlement. The best thing you can do for your children is to learn to negotiate with the other parent and to reach agreement/compromise on important matters concerning your children such as access, money, schooling, etc. One way to do this is by learning to develop a business relationship with your former partner

Developing a 'Business-Like' Relationship
Isolina Ricci (1997) writes about how most of the conflict between parents post-separation is caused by one or both of them still expecting to relate to the other on an intimate level, as if they were still married or in a close intimate relationship. This can lead to great hurt being expressed and unhelpful expectations being created. She argues that the best solution is for parents to withdraw from having an intimate relationship and to create

a new working relationship that is more business-like. It is better to relate to your former partner as if they were an important colleague in a work context. You may not be best friends and you may not be emotionally close, but you are bound together in an extremely important shared business goal – parenting your children. The personal relationship has ended, but the business of parenting continues, and it is crucial that you find a new business-like way of relating. The more you are able to do that, the better for your children. The following are the principles of building an effective business-like relationship with your former partner.

MAINTAIN YOUR INDEPENDENCE AND RESPECT THE OTHER PARENT'S INDEPENDENCE

Although you are co-parents, you also have separate lives and separate homes. Just as in a work setting where business and private lives are kept separate, so it can be in your relationship with your former partner. If achieved, this can be a relief, especially if you have been in constant conflict. Remember, your involvement with your former partner is time-limited and focused on parenting and the needs of your children. In addition, accept the fact that you and the other parent will have different styles of parenting. There will be different rules in each of your houses, different routines and a different way of relating to your children. While you will have to agree on some important matters, it is okay for things to be different and children can cope with this quite well. It is more important to children to see their parents relating respectfully to one another than for every rule to be consistent and agreed.

KEEP YOUR FEELINGS IN CHECK

Don't ask too much about your former partner's personal life and feelings, and don't over-disclose about your own personal matters either. This means that if you feel upset at being alone or feel jealous of your former partner's new relationship, do not talk to them about these feelings, rather set some time aside to share these with a close friend. In addition, don't let your anger or frustration get the better of you. If you do so, you are likely to evoke an angry or defensive response and stop any positive negotiation.

Effective negotiators never lose control of their feelings. They remain calm and put their anger and frustration to one side.

KEEP YOUR COMMUNICATION FOCUSED ON THE PRESENT AND THE NEEDS OF YOUR CHILDREN

When conflict is high it is hard to stay focused on the needs of your children. Parents can get distracted easily by past hurts and other grievances and bring up non-parenting issues instead. It is important that you resist this temptation and that you focus clearly on the present and what you want for your children. Equally, don't take the bait if your former partner presses your buttons and brings up an old argument. Instead, politely refocus the discussion, for example by saying, 'I'm not going to talk about that now, I simply rang to fix a time for me to collect Sue.'

DO COMMUNICATE DIRECTLY AND OPENLY WITH THE OTHER PARENT

If you have something to say to the other parent that is relevant to the business of co-parenting, then it is important that you communicate this to them directly, either face to face, by telephone, or even by note. Be wary of communicating indirectly by asking someone else to tell them, and it is certainly unfair, as previously mentioned, to use your children as go-betweens. If you need to change a time of a visit, then ring the other parent to discuss this. If this is difficult you could consider writing a note, but don't ask your children to negotiate on your behalf.

Negotiating with the Other Parent

Learning to negotiate with the other parent over important parenting issues, and coming to acceptable agreements about your children's care, is a crucial step in helping them cope with the separation. As stated before, this is often very difficult to achieve, and we suggest a number of negotiation principles that can help this come about.

PICK A GOOD TIME TO NEGOTIATE

Negotiation works best when you are both calm and have enough time to talk. If you have an issue that you need to negotiate with the other parent about, think carefully about when and where to do this. It is probably not a good time to raise it when you are angry or upset. For example, if the other parent is consistently late picking up the children for access, leaving you dealing with anxious and waiting children, confronting them on the doorstep in front of the children, when you are both pressured and your anger is heightened, is probably not a good idea. It might be better to plan to ring later about it or to ask, 'I need to talk to you about the collecting arrangements, when would be a good time to ring?'

LISTEN FIRST

Effective negotiators always take steps to understand and appreciate the other person's point of view before they communicate their own thoughts. This can be hard if you're in conflict all the time. The most important skill in reducing conflict is listening. If you can listen and show you appreciate the other parent's point of view, then they are more likely to listen and take on board your views also. Listening is not about agreeing or giving up your own position, it is simply about understanding. For example, even though you feel financially stretched paying child support and living in a small apartment, you can still appreciate the financial burden of your former partner living as a single parent. Or even though you deal with the children all day long and feel burdened by this, you can still appreciate the distance your former partner has to travel in traffic to get there on time.

GIVE YOUR VIEW RESPECTFULLY

When giving your point of view, make sure you do it in a way that is respectful and assertive. Avoid harassing, threatening or insulting the other parent and try not to blame or overcriticise. None of these tactics will help matters, but they can be very damaging. Be positive and calm when you express your point of view, take responsibility for your feelings and express what you want to happen. Consider the following examples:

INEFFECTIVE: You're deliberately changing the access times to try and stop me seeing the kids. You've no right. (*Attacking and blaming 'you' message.*)

EFFECTIVE: The change of time doesn't suit me because of my work. I would prefer if we kept the time the same. (*Gives clear explanation and states what he/she wants.*)

INEFFECTIVE: You're so inconsiderate. You never think to get the children to do their homework on the weekend. It's just all fun for you, and I'm left to force them to do it when they're tired. (*Sarcastic, blaming.*)

EFFECTIVE: Listen, I appreciate that you like to do fun things over the weekend with the kids, but it is important that they do their homework as well. Can you arrange a time to do it with them over the weekend? (*States positive first and then makes a clear, reasonable request.*)

THINK OF MUTUALLY BENEFICIAL SOLUTIONS

The final stage of negotiation is to try to come up with solutions and agreements that are beneficial to both you and the other parent. This is very different from gaining a victory over your former partner or proving that they were wrong. Both of these strategies are shortsighted, making it unlikely that your former partner will co-operate in the future. It is, rather, about finding a way of accommodating both your points of view through a solution that you both accept. In the homework example above, for instance, the parents may come up with the following solution: the first parent does some of the homework with the children before they go away on the weekend, the second parent makes sure to complete it with the children on Sunday before they return to the first parent, who arranges a quiet evening in with them. With this solution, parents share in both the fun and the responsibilities of caring for the children. Finding mutually beneficial solutions is often simply about negotiating satisfactory compromises. For example, a father may agree to let the children have 'his' Saturday with the mother, because she has a special family event. But the mother agrees to return the favour the following month when the father wants to take the children away for an extended weekend.

How to Negotiate when the Other Parent is Unreasonable

In the hurt and bitterness of separation, it is very common for parents to behave unreasonably at times, either by refusing to negotiate or by becoming excessively hostile. During those times it can be important to take a break from negotiations and to try again at another time. In time, strong emotions can settle down and people can become more open to discussion.

If you have difficulty talking directly to each other, you can seek the help of a professional mediation service (see Useful Resources at the end of the book). A mediator will meet with both of you and try to help you come up with a working parenting agreement. In addition, you can also seek legal help via a solicitor and go to court to resolve your dispute. A judge can establish a schedule of contact or strongly encourage you to go to mediation, or request an outside expert to assess what is best for your children. Sometimes, in circumstances of high conflict, a court order can be helpful in fixing the times of contact and the amount of access where parents are unable to negotiate this directly. One should be cautious about using the court system excessively, however, as the adversarial nature of court can aggravate rather than reduce conflict.

In a minority of cases (for example, when there has been abuse or physical violence) it may not be possible or advisable for you to negotiate with your former partner. In those cases, you could seek the support of professional services such as those listed at the back of the book.

BEING A SINGLE PARENT

The Challenges

Post-separation, many parents (usually mothers) suddenly find themselves in the role of single parent; they are now almost solely responsible for the daily care of their children, with all the struggles and stresses this brings. While children are not necessarily worse off because they live in a single-parent family (and indeed there can be advantages if the new arrangement relieves children of being in an excessively conflictual home situation), single parenthood brings considerable challenges and stresses:

» Reduced income, due to the increased childcare costs and the need to maintain two homes.

» Loss of an ally and co-parent. The multiple demands of busy family life still have to be managed, but now with one less pair of hands.

» Less personal and social time for you. There will be fewer breaks and opportunities for you to relax and look after your own needs, even though the parenting demands on you have increased.

» Managing the children's distress alone. Children who are upset and angry at their parents' separation often only express their feelings to the parent caring for them on a daily basis. You are likely to get the brunt of their distress and have to deal with many discipline issues alone.

Rising to the Challenge

WORK CONSTRUCTIVELY WITH THE OTHER PARENT

As discussed in the last chapter, there are clear advantages to maintaining a civil and business-like relationship with your former partner. Children do best when the live-away parent remains supportively involved and in contact with them. For example, research has shown that children from single-parent families (headed by the mother) do better academically when fathers are actively involved in their children's schooling, for example by attending parent–teacher meetings. In simple terms, children do better when they have two concerned and interested parents involved in their lives.

In addition, the involvement of the other parent can have advantages for you in reducing the burden of being a single parent. If your former partner takes a more extensive childcare role, then you will have more time to yourself to recharge and to pursue your own social interests. Second, you will have reduced childcare costs because you don't have to pay a babysitter and because live-away parents who remain emotionally involved in their children's lives are much more likely to pay child support and to support their children financially as they become adults (e.g. when they go to college). Finally, children who are in contact with the other parent (and this is particularly the case for boys and their fathers) can be helped settle more quickly after the separation and may be less likely to have discipline problems.

For all these reasons, it is worth working hard to facilitate the involvement of the other parent in your children's lives even though you have separated. While this is not always within your control (many live-away parents drift apart from their children despite the best intentions of the custodial parent), certainly don't put up any unnecessary obstacles to the other parent remaining involved. For example, you may be tempted to punish your former partner by restricting access, but this does not serve your children's or your own interests in the long term. Even if your former partner, in your view, took on few childcare responsibilities when they were living at home, this does not mean that they could not take on parenting responsibilities when separated. Most live-away parents can quickly learn these tasks in the period following separation.

It is also your right to insist that your former partner takes on their fair share of the childcare responsibilities. It is generally the best for your child, and relieves you of some of the burdens of being a single parent. For ideas on how to negotiate with your former partner about co-parenting, see the previous chapter.

BE ORGANISED

Parents generally need to be organised, but single parents who head up households really need to be organised. It has already been suggested that separated parents should try and develop a business-like relationship with each other, but it can also help to think of the family as a business. Businesses need to plan ahead and so do single parents!

Each evening draw up a plan for the next day. Note down which jobs are essential, which are desirable, and which can really wait. Daily planning will help you avoid things like the morning scramble. It may also help with your own sleep because you don't need to lay awake trying to remember all the tasks you have to do the next day!

Once a week, sit down with the children and plan for the medium term. Medium-term planning means you don't lose sight of the bigger picture and the less frequent but important family events like holiday and birthday planning. Successful businesses have good filing systems. They know where to find important information. In families, a lot of time can be lost and plenty of hassle experienced in looking for bills, forms and receipts – so make sure to keep track of everything.

MAINTAIN THE QUALITY OF YOUR PARENTING

Under the stress of single parenthood, it is easy to let the quality of your parenting slip. You may suddenly find yourself having to be both mother and father to the children, being nurturing and kind as well as firm and authoritarian. This can be difficult if you deferred some of these roles to your former partner, for example, if they were the main nurturer, or the parent who looked after discipline. In addition, children can present a lot of discipline problems after their parents' separation and need firm and loving parenting more than ever. So it is really important that you get the support you need to maintain the quality of your parenting. This includes setting individual time aside to listen, talk and play with your children, being consistent in your rules and routines, and being calm and firm when you enforce rules. See the earlier chapter on Helping Children Cope (p. 21), or some of the further reading listed at the end for more ideas.

SEEK THE SUPPORT YOU NEED

It is hard being a parent alone, so it is really important that you seek the support you need. Extended family members, friends and neighbours can all be great sources of practical and emotional support as you take on the task of single parenthood. You might also find a lot of resources (such as parents' groups or family resource centres) in your local community that may be helpful to you. For example, some parents cope by sharing tasks such as the school run with other parents. A good idea is to make a list of the supports you need, what is available and who can help.

As stated before, don't forget to work constructively with the children's other parent to ensure they take on some of the childcare responsibilities. This is often the best arrangement for your children, who gain contact with their 'live-away' parent while you can pursue other things.

Finally, it is also reasonable to expect children, especially the older ones, to play a role in looking after household responsibilities. You may even find that this sharing of responsibility gives the children a sense of importance and enhanced worth. Sharing the responsibility may also help to bond the new and smaller unit and may give everybody a better sense of stability, which is probably much needed following the transition to being a single-parent family.

Tricky Situations and What to Do About Them

WHEN YOU ROW EVERY TIME YOU MEET THE OTHER PARENT

Sometimes separation and divorce can be very messy. The feelings of hurt and anger can last well beyond the actual split and spill out each time you meet. If the other parent is to continue to play a role in the child's life – and usually this is a good idea – then you really need to work on creating a civil, business-like relationship with them. Here are some useful ideas for you to try. First, organise that the hand-over of children occurs in a public place. This reduces the chances of there being an open row. Second, you may find it better to deliver rather than collect the children. Delivering leaves less time for hanging around, and thus less space for that row to develop. Third, communicate important information – changes in the child's medication, the time of football practice – in writing, but keep it factual. We have already emphasised how important it is to avoid using the children as the message carrier and for them to be kept clear of parental rows. Finally, if difficulties persist, it is worth seeking professional help in the form of a family counsellor or a mediator who can help you and your former partner to come to a workable agreement (see the previous chapter for more ideas).

WHEN THE OTHER PARENT IS UNRELIABLE

Children in separated families can be hurt and can get very angry when their parents fail to keep to arrangements. When their live-away parent doesn't turn up on a regular basis children often conclude that they are not loved by him/her.

If access arrangements are not working out then the first step is for the parents to try and discuss the issues and to negotiate a different arrangement that suits everyone. If it is not possible to negotiate a more reliable arrangement with the other parent you should negotiate a 'Plan B' with the children. Plan B might specify how long they would wait for the live-away parent to arrive and what alternative activities are available should the promised arrival not occur. This sort of Plan B approach can often provide much relief for children and help them cope with the uncertain access arrangements.

In many cases it is not possible to negotiate satisfactory visiting arrangements with the live-away parent. As stated earlier, many live-away parents can drift out of their children's lives despite the best intentions of the custodial parent to maintain their involvement. In these situations it is important to be sensitive to your children's feelings. They may feel upset, disappointed and angry at the other parent's lack of involvement and will need you to listen and support them. Be careful not to express your own angry feelings about the other parent by bad-mouthing them, but rather try and listen and give a balanced account of the reasons for their other parent's lack of involvement. In addition, be open to the fact that the level of contact between your children and the other parent may change over time. For example, it is common as their own circumstances change for live-away parents to try to restart or increase contact with their children.

It is important that you are open to this idea and available to negotiate it carefully in the best interests of your children.

Equally, your children may wish to initiate contact with the live-away parent themselves, for example, by writing a letter, sending an email or making a telephone call. Indeed, it is very common for children as they become older to become interested in the parent they have lost touch with and to want to make new efforts to contact them. As the custodial parent, your children will need your support and guidance if contact with the live-away parent is to restart in a helpful way.

SHOULD I GET A JOB OUTSIDE THE HOME?

There are pros and cons. Work outside the home can certainly provide benefits: you get to socialise with other adults; you acquire a new role in life; and work brings cash and easier access to credit facilities. But there are disadvantages too. Just arranging good childcare can be a difficult issue for many working parents, never mind being able to afford it. There can be other work-related expenses too, for example the cost of transport to and from work, the cost of clothes for work and eating your lunch out. And if you work outside the home the housework doesn't go away. You have to squeeze it in at another time. You also have to plan for what happens if your child is sick. It would be wise to check carefully whether the overall benefits to you of working are not outweighed by the loss of financial benefits from the State. Some parents find a happy medium in finding part-time work or a job with flexible hours that they can balance around their busy life as a single parent.

ARE THERE TIMES WHEN I SHOULD SEEK HELP FROM PROFESSIONALS?

The simple answer is yes. If you've tried negotiating with the other parent on important issues and had insufficient success, then maybe you should think about going to a professional counsellor or mediator or consulting a solicitor. If you feel you are not managing, and are getting overwhelmed, then talk to a reliable friend or a sensible relative, or seek some professional support, perhaps from your GP. If the children are really not settling, then maybe they need to see a counsellor with you or on their own.

BEING A LIVE-AWAY PARENT

Post-separation, the most common living arrangement is for the children to live with one parent (usually the mother) and for the other parent (usually the father) to live away, but to have contact with the children. This level of contact can vary greatly. In the chaotic time just after separation contact can be sporadic or even cease for a period (sadly, just when children, especially younger ones, need most reassurance from the parent who has left). Over time the situation can stabilise and many live-away parents are successful in achieving good quality, regular contact with their children. It is often difficult for this contact to be maintained, however, and there is a tendency for it to wane and to eventually stop. In research studies, nearly half of the parents who live away from their children post-separation lose contact altogether with their children within a few years.

While these parents are often characterised as selfish or not caring of their children, this does not take into account the obstacles and difficulties live-away parents face when they attempt to maintain supportive contact. Many struggle with their own personal pain and the practical difficulties such as finding accommodation and tight finances. They often find themselves at great disadvantage in the courts, with their former partner who lives with the children holding all the cards. Others feel great guilt or hurt at the separation and this prevents them from having contact with the children as this will bring them into contact with their former partner. Others wonder if they have anything of value to offer their children and often think their children would be better off without them.

Despite these obstacles, however, many live-away parents are successful in creating a stable situation where they work with their former partner to have regular quality contact with their children, and are a positive influence as their children grow up. In the next section we outline some important principles in achieving this.

Staying connected with your children and supportively involved in their lives is difficult at the best of times, even when you live with the other parent. It becomes especially difficult if you are a live-away parent and you have to work harder to maintain a positive connection.

Co-operate with Your Former Partner

We have already emphasised how important it is for you to develop a co-operative, 'business-like' relationship with your former partner for the sake of your children. This is especially the case if you are the live-away parent. It will be very difficult for you to maintain a quality relationship with your children unless, on some level, you have the support of your former partner, who is living with your children daily and has a strong influence on them. Perhaps the single biggest reason live-away parents stop having contact with their children is due to ongoing conflict with the children's live-in parent. It is important to take steps to reduce this conflict and to negotiate with your former partner. As described in the last chapter, this is not about giving in to your former partner on every issue or accepting unreasonable demands, but about understanding their perspective, persisting in communicating your point of view and seeking compromise and mutually beneficial solutions.

Live-away parents often feel they are in a weaker position than that of the other parent, who can call all the shots. In such instances, there is the option of seeking support from the court system. Except in exceptional cases, a judge will grant 'reasonable' access to a live-away parent and in many instances they are prepared to consider shared custody, giving parents equal responsibility. Though we are wary of the adversarial nature of courts, in many high-conflict situations a court order regularising contact arrangements can help settle and stabilise matters. Even when a court order has been granted, it is still important to work on building a co-operative civil relationship with your former partner. If you find yourself constantly fighting with your former partner, you are indirectly fighting your children, who more often than not are caught in the middle of this conflict.

KEEP YOUR PROMISES

Keeping promises with children is important. It becomes especially so when you live away from them following a separation. When you lived with your children you might have been flexible or loose about when you would take them out or read them a bedtime story. After separation it is important to be much more definite and consistent. Children can be devastated if their parent is late or, worse still, does not turn up for an agreed activity, or forgets to make the promised telephone call. The regularity of these actions help children feel secure and loved and ensure you remain connected and involved. This is why it is important to only make promises that you can keep. Don't arrange to call at a time when you are likely to be busy, or pick a visit time that is impossible due to a lengthy travel time.

If you cannot keep contact time or are going to be late, tell your child in advance and make alternative arrangements. It's also important to say sorry if you have let your child down. This can be very helpful to children in showing how seriously you rate spending time with them.

It can be helpful to plan your time together in advance, for when you do meet. You could chat with your child about what you are going to do, and even draw up a master list of activities you both enjoy or places you both like to visit. Focus on having a pleasant relaxed time together rather than a frantic rush to fit everything in, and remember, it doesn't have to be expensive to be fun – most children value their parents' time and attention more than anything else.

Be a Responsible Parent

When you do see your children it is natural to want to try and make it a fun and enjoyable experience, full of nice trips and activities. However, it is also important not to shirk on parenting responsibilities such as helping children with homework, setting rules and ensuring they go to bed on time. Your children will respect you greatly as they grow up if you take your fair share of the responsible side of parenting (as well as the fun side). Equally, this is the best way to co-operate with their live-in parent. For example, it is very common for children to have some behavioural problems post-separation and to take a lot of their anger out on the parent they live with. If your former partner is struggling with a discipline issue, don't use this as an opportunity to blame them or to point out how you would be better at handling the problem, but support them instead. Work together to solve the problem through adopting a common discipline approach. If as a father you discover that your son is rude and aggressive to his mother, you could, on discussion with her, sit down with him and explain that you don't tolerate such behaviour, that you want him to find other ways to express his anger and that he must be more respectful to his mother. Similarly, if your daughter is falling behind on her grades, make sure to schedule time to do homework with her when she visits.

Be Creative About How You Stay in Touch

Face-to-face contact isn't the only way to keep in touch with your children; there are many other creative ways, listed below, that can be very valuable, especially if you live far away from your children and regular in-person contact is not possible.

TEXTING/EMAIL

Nowadays it is fairly easy to keep in contact with people, even over long distances. Texting and email means you can be in daily contact, keeping up to date with what is happening in children's lives, answering questions and reassuring them about what's happening in your life, all at minimal expense. Make sure to agree the mode in which you communicate with the child's other parent.

PHONE/SKYPE/VIDEO PHONE

The phone is better still and you should try to phone children regularly at an agreed time each week. The advent of video phones and Skype makes this all easier and the conversation more rich as you can see as well as hear your children. Some children, particularly younger ones, find it hard to talk over the phone and wonder what they should chat to you about. It is worth noting down topics before you call, for example who they are meeting/playing with, how school is going, what they have been doing in their spare time. With older children, you and they can keep a diary through the week noting down things you want to tell each other. When phoning, make sure you are in good form and keep the atmosphere upbeat. Keep the appointed time sacred and don't change it as it is the regular routine of the call that makes the contact effective. During the call, be open to what your children may be concerned about and what they want to discuss with you. Be careful not to load them with your worries, concerns and regrets and focus on their needs.

POSTAL MAIL

In the electronic era it is perhaps even more pleasant to get something through the post. Buy a selection of cards in one go and then you can send them at intervals. Sending small gifts in the post when your children are not expecting them can reassure the child that they are in your thoughts. If you provide a pack of stamped addressed envelopes for the child to send notes to you, this may also help them to feel more in touch.

Other ways to stay connected:

- » For younger children you can tape/video record yourself reading bedtime stories.
- » With older children you can write or invent stories for them to read, which you can send them in the post or email to them. Ask them to add to the stories.
- » Chat about books you and the child are reading at the same time or about a TV programme or a match you have both watched.
- » Go out and buy copies of the books your child is reading in school or the games they like so you know what they are doing and thinking about.
- » Send daily postcards when you go on holidays.
- » Come up with a shared project or interest with each of your children that you can share with them even from afar – this could be as simple as following the same football team or supporting them in a special school project or activity.

» Keep a diary of what is happening in your life, with pictures of their extended family and events they may not be attending. You can share this periodically with them when you are in contact and keep it safe for them as they get older.

» Use photos – tell the child where you have put theirs and maybe take photos when you have outings together for them to keep as a reminder.

Whether you live far away from your children or not, creative ways of staying in touch can be extremely valuable in getting the message across to them that you are there for them, that you are thinking of them and that you love them.

Don't be Disheartened by Rejection

Live-away parents often become disheartened when their children seem at times uninterested in their visits or contact. You might go to great effort to ring at a certain time only to be told by your daughter that she wants to return to watching her favourite TV programme. Or you might be upset that your children never write back to your weekly letters and cards and be tempted to stop writing. It is important to remember, however, that this is quite normal. Even in 'live-together' families, children can take their parents' attention for granted. It is quite normal for older children and teenagers to want to spend more time with their friends and to become more interested in activities outside the family.

What is important is that you don't take this apparent lack of interest personally or interpret it as a sign to stop making efforts to keep in contact. Rather it is important to be flexible about contact, making an effort to fit it in with all the other activities and interests in your children's lives. In addition, it is unreasonable to expect young children (and even teenagers) to make efforts to contact you or to always respond to your initiatives. It is your responsibility to keep contact going and this will stand to you in the long term as your children become adults and they realise the efforts you made to be there for them and to stay involved in their lives.

Be Patient if Restarting Contact

For different reasons, many live-away parents lose contact with their children. They can find themselves in the position of wondering whether to restart contact and how to go about this. This is a very delicate issue. Children can be very angry at a parent who they perceive as having abandoned them and, depending on their age, who may also have moved on to create a new life for themselves. In restarting contact it is important to go slow and to be patient. Think through what role you are prepared to have in your child's life and don't restart contact if you are not able to maintain it or become supportively involved.

Before resuming contact, you will first have to discuss with your child's live-in parent about how to do it, and this can take some time and delicate negotiation (either directly, via mediation or via court). Once this is done, it may be a good idea to restart contact with your children in stages, by writing to them for a period before meeting them. Whatever way you start contact, be prepared for the fact that you may have to apologise for not keeping contact in the past, and remember that it will take time to rebuild their trust and a new relationship with them.

NEW RELATIONSHIPS AND STEP-FAMILIES

After separation, many parents go on to form relationships with new partners. It is perfectly reasonable that parents should have a social life and that they move on in this way. However, introducing new significant people into children's lives is a tricky process and can be fraught with difficulties. Below are a number of guidelines to help you take your children's needs into account as you embark on dating, making new relationships and forming step-families.

Starting to Date and Make New Relationships

Reassure the children repeatedly, by word and deed, that dating doesn't affect your love for them or mean they are taking second place. Children who have experienced separation and divorce are naturally concerned about being abandoned and about losing you. If you are dating, then there is even more need for you to set aside special time to remain well connected with your children. Don't jump feet first into a new relationship. Take it slowly. It has to be a package deal. If the new partner isn't keen on children or the idea of an instant family then it's best to call a halt early on.

Children shouldn't be present when you are dating a new person. Quite apart from the fact that it is about adults relating, the relationship may not last, and exposing children to a string of different partners leads them to feel confused and uncertain. It's best early on that your dating takes place outside the home, and only in the home when the children are away (for example, staying with the other parent). Give your children plenty of time to get used to the idea that you have a new partner before the first face-to-face meeting takes place.

When your children have met your new partner, be open to their opinions and listen to what they have to say about the new person. It is understandable that they may have very mixed feelings about there being another adult in your life. You may even be introducing this new person before the children have completely sorted out issues to do with their other parent and your separation. Accept that teenagers may not want to spend much time with parents, let alone with their parent's new partner.

Step-Families

Adults and children who join together as a step-family face significant challenges. Learning to live and get on with a new set of people can be fraught with 'teething problems'. Children can feel jealous at having to share their parents, or left out and insecure in the new living arrangements. Becoming a happy and harmonious step-family isn't easy and special planning and preparation is required. A useful first question for the adults to ask is what does it look like from where the children are standing?

Children joining a new step-family bring with them the experience of family breakdown and possibly of marital conflict, and certainly a sense of loss. The new union may mean that they have to move away from their familiar friends, from their old school, neighbourhood and extended family.

Children joining a new family may also be required to share their space with the step-parent's own children. At the very least they will now clearly be sharing their parent with another adult. For older children this may also mean giving up some of the more grown-up responsibility they took on, or were given, when their biological parents' relationship broke down. For all children, a new union is further proof that their biological parents will not be getting back together gain. That realisation may provoke another bout of grieving.

As if these changes weren't enough, children may feel that they share some of the responsibility for the breakdown of the relationship between their biological parents. They may fear being rejected or disliked by the new step-parent, and worry about the implications of that for their relationship with the custodial parent. Children are likely to have had little or no say in whether this new family should form. They know that things can go badly wrong in families and here they are entering another.

What Can the Adults do to Help?

THE CUSTODIAL PARENT

TAKE IT SLOW AND BE UNDERSTANDING

Your children may be initially reluctant and unsure about the new family arrangements and will need a lot of time to come to terms with it. Listen to their feelings and wishes and, as far as possible, take these into account when you plan for the future.

SUPPORT YOUR CHILDREN'S RELATIONSHIP WITH THE OTHER PARENT

Don't see the family arrangements as an opportunity to 'cut loose' or reduce contact with the other parent. Children often need a lot of reassurance during this time that their other parent will continue to be involved in their lives. It's a big help if you can maintain a good co-parenting relationship and communicate and negotiate directly with the other parent to facilitate the children keeping in touch.

MAKE SURE YOU SPEND INDIVIDUAL TIME WITH YOUR CHILDREN

Many children spend less individual time with their birth parent in a new family and miss this greatly. Don't insist that your new partner or new step-children become involved in all family activities you spend with your children. Set aside special time and activities when you can be alone with your children to listen and talk to them and to simply enjoy each other's company. In preparing to form a step-family, it can be helpful to have a series of family talks with the 'original family' (i.e. you and your children) before introducing your new partner and step-children to the discussions.

WORK ON DEVELOPING A GOOD RELATIONSHIP WITH YOUR NEW PARTNER

It is helpful if your children see that you have a supportive relationship with your new partner and that it leads to more harmony for all. If you are going to have an argument with your new partner then try to hold it until the children are not around. Arguments may be particularly worrying for them if they were associated with the breakdown of your relationship with their other parent. Open communication between the new couple about their own parenting style, standards and expectations, and particularly good communication and problem solving about how their differing styles can be merged, is essential to success. Mutual support for each other creates a climate of security for the children. How the new couple negotiate and resolve their differences can also serve as a very useful learning experience for children, and a model for how the children can usefully play their part in forming the new family.

THE LIVE-AWAY PARENT

ACCEPT THE ROLE OF THE NEW STEP-PARENT IN YOUR CHILDREN'S LIVES

It is very helpful if you can accept that there is now a new adult in your child's life and that you do not compete with or be negative about them. Your child should feel free to mention their new step-parent without having to fear your reaction. Even more than this, your child may need your support to form a relationship with the step-parent and to know that they are not being disloyal to you by doing so. Remember, the arrival of a step-parent can have a number of advantages for your child. By providing support to the other parent, the step-parent can often help create more security and stability for your child, and indeed may form a supportive friendship with your child that is another resource for him/her.

MAINTAIN YOUR OWN SUPPORTIVE INVOLVEMENT

Though the arrival of a new step-parent does bring changes, it need not drastically alter your relationship with your children. Though you may need to negotiate with the other parent about the new living arrangements and be flexible about how you maintain contact, you should work hard to ensure you remain involved. Rather than 'backing off' to give the family space, children often need you more during these times, and they can become very distressed when parents do not visit or phone at the agreed time. Show by your actions as well as your words that your feelings for your children have not and will not change.

THE NEW STEP-PARENT

TAKE TIME TO BUILD A RELATIONSHIP WITH YOUR PARTNER'S CHILDREN

As a step-parent you will have a very different relationship with your partner's children to what they have with their birth parents. While young children may begin to relate to you in a parenting role, older children are likely to have much more mixed feelings. Many children will see you not as their step-parent but as their mother's or father's new partner. Give the children space to work out their feelings and don't put them under any pressure. Respect their relationship with their live-away parent and avoid competing or trying to replace this parent's involvement. Young children are capable of developing good, strong attachments with both types of parents. However, a good relationship between a child and a new step-parent will take time to develop. It would be nice if happy families could be created instantly, but that's not what happens in the real world. Some experts suggest that the process can take between two and five years.

INITIALLY BECOME A 'SUPPORTIVE FRIEND' TO YOUR NEW STEP-CHILDREN

A good way to start is to try and build a 'supportive friendship' with your step-child. Don't immediately leap into the role of being a parent, but spend some time getting to know them and understanding what their concerns and interests are. It can be a good idea to try and develop a shared interest with them, but let this evolve naturally. It can be much harder with older children and teenagers who are unsure about what type of relationship they want to have with you. Expect initial rejection and don't take it personally. Be patient and persistent in trying to become friends with them.

DON'T GET TOO INVOLVED INITIALLY IN DISCIPLINE

Children, especially the older ones, are likely to resent it if you immediately take on a disciplinarian role with them. It is best initially to leave this to their birth parents and for you to adopt a supportive role to your partner and the children as they work out discipline issues. As you develop a more trusting relationship with the children, you will be able to assume a more central parenting role, especially if the children are younger. With older children and teenagers, however, who are already moving towards independence, this may not happen, and it is best to simply maintain a supportive role.

WORK ON DEVELOPING A GOOD RELATIONSHIP WITH YOUR NEW PARTNER

A new step-parent may feel like an outsider at first, realising that they are not part of much of the history and shared experience of their new partner and his/her children. Time and experience will create a new, shared family history. In the meantime, it is particularly important for the new couple to work hard on strengthening their own bond so that there is a secure base from which they and the children can build this shared positive experience.

Moving Things Forward

People enter step-families with a history of traditions, experiences and expectations. These may not be immediately apparent. From time to time the new family members may be quite surprised to find that much of what they take for granted is not universally accepted as the way to do things. It is likely that new rituals, rules and ways of behaving will have to be developed.

Getting to Know One Another

It is really important to set aside time for the new family members to talk, share and to get to know one another. This can be done by having a sit-down meal without the TV, or by being around to chat when the children come in from school. Regular family meetings can also be very helpful. These meetings can be used to discuss routines and family rules, to solve problems, to plan fun activities such as holidays and trips and to chat and 'check in' with one another. Children should be allowed to have their say, express their needs and feelings, make their own suggestions and have a real input into the final agreements. Family meetings can be really important in helping children feel appreciated and supported and in giving them a sense of belonging. Overall, such meetings can help everyone stay connected and involved in each other's lives and can bring the family closer together.

PART 2
Common Problems and Issues

EMOTIONAL UPSET AND BEHAVIOUR PROBLEMS

My thirteen-year-old son blames me and not his father for the separation

Q. *I separated from my husband just under two years ago, mainly due to his drinking and gambling. It has been a hard couple of years, though things are a lot better now. My ex has got his act together. He lives with his mother, has stopped drinking and gambling and sees the children regularly. The problem is that my oldest son, who turned thirteen last month, has become really cheeky and disrespectful to me at home. He has been really critical of me and everything I do. In particular, he doesn't like me going out to socialise and makes negative comments that I am 'too old' to go out, etc. It's weird, but it reminds me of the way that his dad used to try to control me during the bad times. I thought a lot of the problems were his age and teen hormones but then we had a big row last weekend, and he blurted out that he didn't know why I 'threw Dad out of the house'. I saw red and blew my top. I was furious to be blamed for what was really his dad's fault. Now I feel guilty for shouting at him and I am also really annoyed at his dad, who seems to be having conversations with my son that somehow make him out to be the innocent party. What should I do?*

A. Parenting an adolescent can have its ups and downs at the best of times, and in the context of parental separation it can bring special challenges. During the adolescent years children can re-experience some of the hurt and confusion they might have originally felt about their parents' separation. As they can now think in more complicated ways, new questions can emerge for them as to why their parents separated and they can feel a divided sense of loyalty more acutely than before. Frequently, to make sense of what happens, they can feel they have to take a side or judge one of their parents as being at fault for the separation.

As they are dealing with their own emerging sexuality, adolescents can be uncomfortable with their parents starting new relationships at this point in their lives. This could be the source of his criticism of your socialising.

BEING UNDERSTANDING BUT INSISTING ON RESPECT

While, of course, you can appreciate your son's upset and confusion, it is not okay for him to be disrespectful or aggressive towards you. While you can understand some of his discomfort about you dating, it is not acceptable for him to try to control your life or to feel he can negatively comment about your social life. To help him, the key is to encourage him to express his feelings, worries and upsets, but in a way that is respectful to both you and his father. At thirteen he probably does need more information about the separation, and teenagers appreciate being spoken to in more of an adult way about the circumstances of the separation, as they are better able to understand.

PRESENT THE TWO SIDES TO THE SEPARATION

Use the fact that you had a row as an opportunity to approach him at a better time to raise the subject of the separation. Pick a good time when he is calm and open and check in with how he is feeling, for example: 'I am sorry we had a row the other day, but you raised some important worries about how your dad and I separated.'

Try to listen without judgement to what he says and encourage him to share his feelings. When you do explain the circumstances of the separation to him, try to do it in a way that is factual and does not blame either you or his father, or that at least is compassionate to both of you. If you can, a good idea is to first present your perspective on how the marriage ended and then to also present his father's perspective. You may have different views, but that is all right. During this conversation you can emphasise the importance of respect and remind him of the importance of respecting you as his mother, whatever his feelings.

INVOLVE HIS FATHER IN THIS CONVERSATION

If possible, the ideal is for this information to come from both you and his father. You don't say how communication is between you and his father at the moment, but it is important to tell his father about what happened and to seek his support in resolving things. As well as your son having individual conversations with you and his father about the separation, it might be useful if the three of you could sit down and go over things together, at least initially. That way your son will see you as working together as parents and he will feel less pressure to judge or to take a side. Finally, remember that your son is starting his teen years, which can be a bumpy ride for teens and parents alike. Though he might be pulling away, think of how you can stay connected with him. Prioritise and build on the times when you do get on well with him, whether this is chats before bed, going for a walk or even watching a favourite TV programme together.

My eight-year-old daughter won't do anything I tell her and is really acting up since our separation

Q. *I have recently separated from my husband after ten years of marriage. We have an eight-year-old daughter who lives with me but sees her father every other day for an hour or so, and she stays over one night a week with him. In the past couple of weeks, she has been really acting up and won't do anything I tell her. I seem to be shouting at her all the time and it's really upsetting. I feel like a bad mother and that I can't even control my own child. She seems to behave for everyone else, and her father does not seem to be having the same problems. To be honest, he and her grandparents spoil her (he is living with his parents) and do all the nice stuff, and I'm the one left carrying the can – I have to get her to school, do homework, etc. I don't know if her misbehaviour is to do with the separation – she was upset for the first week when her father left but then settled once she realised things had not changed too much for her and that she would still be seeing everyone.*

A. Children frequently act up and display more misbehaviour when their parents separate and there can be different reasons for this. Sometimes, it is due to the child's distress at their parents' separation and represents their means of expressing their feelings. It can also be due to the parents' distress post-separation, as they might be dealing with their own upset at the break-up or be experiencing more pressure by having to parent alone and so on.

CHILDREN'S DIVIDED SENSE OF LOYALTY AFTER SEPARATION
At the heart of these problems is often the child's divided sense of loyalty when they can feel they have 'chosen' one parent over the other. Children can wonder who is to blame for the separation, sometimes blaming one parent more than the other – and in some situations blaming themselves. Frequently, as in your circumstances, it is the parent doing the day-to-day caring who gets the brunt of the anger, as the child can be on their best behaviour for the parent they see less (and who has less responsibility to oversee homework, routines, etc).

WORKING CONSTRUCTIVELY WITH HER FATHER

There is, however, a lot you can do to improve the situation. First, it is important to work constructively as co-parents with your ex-husband. If possible, it is a good idea to discuss the problems you're having with your daughter and to seek his support in solving them. For example, it would help if he explained to his daughter that even if she is upset she should still behave respectfully to you as her mother. Increasing her father's involvement or making sure he takes on more of the parenting responsibilities – as well as the fun side of parenting – would also help you feel more supported. The more you work constructively together as parents, the less your daughter will feel caught in the middle and the more likely she is to behave. Ideally, it would help if the two of you could sit down together to explain the situation to her, to listen to her feelings and questions, as well as stating how you expect her to behave respectfully towards both of you.

BE UNDERSTANDING OF HOW YOUR DAUGHTER IS FEELING

It is important to be sensitive and understanding of your daughter and how she might be feeling about the separation and what it means to her. Though she might appear fine, it is important to periodically check in with her and ask her how she is doing. Pick a good time to have a chat with her and to listen to how she is feeling.

It can be helpful to raise the issues directly with her, for example: 'Sometimes children can find themselves caught in the middle when their parents separate – do you feel like this?' The key is to be available to listen to her and not to be defensive if she raises some difficult issues. Even if she does not immediately open up about her feelings, letting her know that you are open to hear her when she is ready to talk is important.

INSIST ON RULES AND USE POSITIVE DISCIPLINE

As well as being supportive to your daughter, it is also important to be a parent and to insist that she should adhere to rules and treat you with respect as her mother. When faced by opposition and misbehaviour, it is easy to get caught into ineffective ways of responding, whether this is nagging, criticising or shouting. However, these strategies can make matters worse and easily become vicious cycles.

The key is to learn to interrupt negative rows and to instead use positive discipline, such as calmly setting clear rules and then following through by using consequences and choices rather than anger or criticism. If she is not doing something she is meant to, rather than shouting, think of a good consequence you can use, for example: 'You have five minutes to get ready and if you don't you will lose some of your TV time tonight.'

Positive discipline takes time and patience. There is more information in *Positive Parenting: Bringing Up Responsible, Well-Behaved & Happy Children* (details listed at the end of this book). Though things might be stressful between you and your daughter, it is important to keep the channels of communication open and make sure to include fun and relaxed times in the daily and weekly routine. Creating space in this way makes it easier to manage the conflicts.

TAKE STEPS TO MANAGE YOUR OWN STRESS

Finally, it is important to take steps to manage your own stress and to ensure you are coping personally. Post-separation is a difficult time for parents and children alike. Make a plan to prioritise your own self-care, whether this is getting support from family and friends, or more formally by seeking counselling or connecting with relevant support organisations (see the Useful Resources section at the end of this book for contacts).

My twelve-year-old daughter blames me for the separation because I had an affair

Q. *I split from my wife eight months ago and it is becoming hard to see my twelve-year-old daughter. She seems to be really angry at me and blames me for the separation. The marriage did finally end because I had an affair, but this was after years of problems. To make matters worse, my ex-wife seems to be turning my daughter against me and telling her too much about what happened between us. I don't think it is healthy for my daughter to be so angry and she seems to be pulling away from me (and not wanting to see me much at all). Anytime I talk to her it ends up in a row and makes matters worse. What can I do?*

A. Children often feel very angry when their parents separate and frequently get sucked into the conflict, taking sides and blaming one parent for what happened. This is particularly the case for young teenagers who are beginning to see the world in a more adult way and can make judgements for themselves about what they feel is right or wrong. Many of the teenagers I have worked with have been really hurt by a parent's infidelity and have seen it as a betrayal not just their of mother but of them and the family also. As an adolescent who might think idealistically about relationships and who is coming into an awareness of their own sexuality, this sense of betrayal can be particularly acute. You also have the added dimension of your daughter possibly entering a normal phase of teenage rebellion and being critical of her parents' shortcomings, which might only increase her anger towards you.

LISTEN TO YOUR DAUGHTER WITHOUT BEING DEFENSIVE
The key to helping your daughter is to really listen to her without being defensive. Parents often think that they are listening to their children, but in fact they are using the time to defend what has happened, or to explain their point of view. However, what children really want at this time is for their parents to appreciate their point of view and to hear how they are feeling, however upsetting it is for the parent to hear. Once this happens

then some healing can begin. This means that if your daughter blames you for ending the marriage, rather than immediately defending yourself or blaming her mother, take time to ask her questions like, 'What makes you say that?', or to acknowledge her feelings: 'You sound really angry at me over what happened.'

BE PREPARED TO TAKE RESPONSIBILITY AND APOLOGISE

Many teenagers are grateful if their parents take responsibility for their part in problems and offer an apology as appropriate. For example, depending on what is most bothering your daughter, you can acknowledge that you regret how the marriage ended and say sorry for any hurt it caused her or her mother. Or you can apologise if she feels you were not there for when she needed you.

Always finish such conversations by explaining how much you love her and want to stay involved in her life: 'I'm hoping we can move on from this. I want to have a good relationship with you as your dad.'

GIVE YOUR DAUGHTER A MORE BALANCED ACCOUNT OF THE SEPARATION

Adolescents like it when you treat them in a more grown-up way and give them a balanced account of the separation, according to their level of understanding and in a way that does not compromise your own or your ex-wife's privacy. In simple terms this might mean giving an account of both sides of the separation, first describing things from your own and then from your ex-wife's perspective. It is important to really appreciate the divided loyalty your daughter might be experiencing. Help her to understand what happened without having to choose sides: 'What happened was between your mum and me. I'm sorry if it has upset you.' It is really important to be patient with your daughter and to give her plenty of time to come to terms with what has happened and to re-establish her relationship with you under the new circumstances.

WORK CONSTRUCTIVELY WITH YOUR DAUGHTER'S MOTHER

Try to talk to your ex-wife about the issues and gain her support in helping resolve things with your daughter. Though your ex-wife may still be hurt and angry about the separation herself, she should still see the importance of her daughter continuing to have a good relationship with you as her father and be willing to support this. Practically, this might mean that she would sit down and chat with your daughter and explain that although she is upset, it is still important that she sees you. Giving your daughter 'permission' in this way could be a great help in moving forward. Ideally, it would be great if you and your ex-wife could sit down with your daughter together and discuss the separation and the contact arrangements (the specifics of when your daughter is due to see you, etc.), though you may need to meet separately with your ex-wife first to agree how to do this. Of course, your ex-wife may not be willing to help in this way, though this could change in the course of time. For this reason, keep the channels of communication open and work hard to be constructive. Seek the support of mediation or counselling or other services as appropriate.

Finally, be patient with your daughter. It can take time for everyone to adjust to new circumstances. Stay involved and positive, keep listening and communicating, and over time things should improve.

I'm still upset at the separation – I just can't let go

Q. *Eighteen months ago, my husband left me suddenly after twenty years of marriage. I did not see it coming. We had our problems but no more so than most couples. He said he had been unhappy for years and that he was waiting for the children to be in college before he left (we have a boy and a girl, eighteen and nineteen at the time). They were both devastated by the break-up and refused to see him for a while. I thought things were starting to settle but then I heard he was living with a new, much younger girlfriend. I found myself devastated all over again. I have been crying and feel intensely upset and angry. I put the best part of my life into the marriage and he threw it all away and left us behind. I feel so angry. As a religious person, it was never my plan to be separated and I feel so betrayed. I also keep thinking, what did I do wrong? Should I have spotted things weren't right and done something?*

A. Coming to terms with a marriage ending is difficult at the best of times, but when it is not your decision and you don't see it coming it can be particularly traumatic. Added to the upset and sadness, you can feel confusion as to why the break-up happened, question your own judgement and feel anger at being let down and betrayed by your partner. It is normal to feel that the twenty years you were married have been invalidated and to feel an acute sense of loss, particularly if you have a strong belief in marriage.

It is common to swing between the extreme emotions of being angry at your partner's betrayal to being depressed and questioning why this has happened to you, or ruminating about whether you could have done something to change how things turned out. While time is, of course, a great healer, this pain can return during various life events which remind you of the loss, whether these are weddings, family events or, as in this case, your ex-partner moving on with life without you.

ADULT CHILDREN AND SEPARATION

While many parents leave it until their children are adults to separate, this does not necessarily reduce the upset their children might feel. I have counselled many young adults who are devastated at their parents' separation, experiencing a loss of their sense of home and stability. Though it is, of course, their parents' business, they frequently get caught up in the sense of betrayal and can feel very similar emotions to their parents. In helping your adult children it is important not to overdepend on them as an ally or confidant and to try to give them a balanced and appropriate account of what happened.

In addition, it is helpful to support them in maintaining their relationship with their father, or at least to make sure you are in no way hindering this. It helps if you give them emotional permission not to have to take a side in the dispute and for them to develop their relationship with their father on their own terms.

SEEKING SUPPORT

It is important when you feel upset to reach out and seek help. Gaining the support of another person can make a big difference in helping you cope. Have you considered attending counselling? Most people find it helpful to talk to someone outside the family who can listen and provide support without being caught up in the emotions. A good counsellor will give you time and space to tease out what happened in your marriage, so you can have a balanced understanding that allows you to begin to move on.

You might find group support and meeting people in similar situations more helpful. Have a look at the list of support groups and services listed at the end of this book.

BE PATIENT WITH YOURSELF

It is important to be patient with yourself as you learn to move on. Frequently, when people experience a setback in their coping (such as your upset at your ex-partner moving in with his girlfriend) they beat themselves up and become angry that they still feel this way. This only adds to your pain. An alternative approach is to compassionately accept how you are feeling. Just mindfully notice your emotions ('Oh, there I am feeling upset again – that is understandable') and then let these emotions pass in their own time. Having an expectation that you must feel a certain way is not going to speed up your recovery, but slow it down.

MOVING ON AND BUILDING A NEW LIFE

As well as being accepting and understanding of your emotions, it is also important to move on and build a new life for yourself beyond your marriage. You had probably already started to do this, prior to the recent setback. The key is to set goals that you really want to achieve. Try to see the new opportunities that being single gives you. The ideal is to have a mixture of long-term goals (perhaps starting a new career or finding a new relationship) and short-term ones (such as taking up a hobby or meeting friends). Make a list of all the things you have dreamed of doing and look at how you might start working towards some of these goals.

PROBLEMS WITH CONTACT AND MAINTAINING RELATIONSHIPS WITH PARENTS

My seven-year-old son is very unsettled after weekend contact with his father

Q. *My seven-year-old son spends every second weekend (Friday to Sunday evening) with his father (we separated eighteen months ago). When he comes back from the visits he doesn't talk to me about what went on over the weekend. He is often very tired and upset and it can take a few days for him to get back to his routine. Should I change his access with his father, perhaps shortening the visits? I know his father will object to this.*

A. Even though children benefit from ongoing relationships and contact with both parents after a separation, they are often unsettled at the time leading up to or immediately following a handover between parents. There are a number of different reasons for this. First, depending on the circumstances of the separation, parents themselves can be stressed about the handover – dreading meeting the other parent, however briefly, and there can be lots of practical issues (such as clothes, diet, homework, etc.) that need to be communicated at the time of handover. In addition, children themselves can be stressed at handover – they can pick up on their parents' worries, be anxious about seeing a parent after a gap of time, or they can find it hard to manage the practicalities (not having their belongings in a second home, being away from friends and so on). Furthermore, the handover can bring up painful memories of the separation or remind them of the losses they have experienced. It is important to tune into your son and to think what might be upsetting him. Be patient as he may not be able to fully articulate what is going on for him.

NEGOTIATING CONTACT AND HANDOVERS WITH HIS FATHER

I wouldn't recommend changing the contact without first negotiating this with his father. Shortening the visits may not be the answer as this curtails the benefits of contact with his father. Indeed, some of your son's upset could be caused by the fact that the visits are too infrequent and he would be more settled if his father had more regular contact. However, it is worth thinking through how you can make the transition times more settled for him. Ideally, it would be best if you could discuss these issues directly with his father and agree a plan. The key to negotiation is to focus on a goal centred on your son's needs (How can we help him settle after contact?) and to be constructive and positive (What can we both do to help?). Arrange to meet his father to go through these issues – do seek the help of mediation if such a conversation might be difficult.

AGREEING ON A GOOD ROUTINE FOR CONTACT

Routines are key to helping children settle. Try to agree on this with his father as much as possible. It could be that the routine at his father's house is not helping the situation. For example, it is common that separated fathers, out of a wish to pack as many good experiences in as possible, make the weekend a very intense time for their child. It might be better for his father to include a wind-down period at the end of the visit, or to take on board some of the preparation for school the next day. In addition, you could consider adjusting the contact to shorter more frequent visits, as opposed to a long weekend every two weeks, which would make your son's contact with his father more regular and normal. This is all something to negotiate with his father.

HANDOVER BOOK

A good way to improve handovers is for you and his father to agree to take time to communicate before and after contact about your son's practical arrangements. Understandably, handover can be a pressured time and lots of separated parents find it useful to use a handover book to facilitate this co-parenting conversation. To work well, the book travels with the child and each parent fills it in before handover, describing relevant details that need to be communicated, for example what the child ate, how he slept, whether homework was done, as well as some general details about how the child was feeling. Generally, the book can be viewed by the child and usually they are very happy with the idea as it saves them from being a go-between for sharing news from parent to parent. If a book is not practical, an alternative is to agree on sending a text or email before handover to communicate these details.

TALKING ABOUT WHAT GOES ON DURING THE CONTACT WITH HIS FATHER
It is also very normal for children not to talk much about their visits with the other parent. Often they have a sense of divided loyalty and are worried about saying something that will offend one parent. Many children tell me that they feel under pressure to 'report back', which makes them uncomfortable. Making sure you and your son's father communicate directly with one another about parenting issues lessens this, and the handover book can assist.

While you should give your son his space and privacy, it is also important to encourage him to talk about contact in a normal everyday way, much like how he might talk about being at school. Adopting a relaxed approach is the best way. It can help to ask specific rather than general questions, for example: 'Your father said that you went to a football match. How was the game?' Encouraging normal chit-chat can be very helpful in opening up conversation.

Finally, take a long-term view. Generally the stress of handovers diminishes for children as they get older, settle into a routine and become reassured by the support of both their parents.

How can I help my three-year-old daughter restart contact with her father?

Q. Could you provide guidance as to how to help my daughter, who is three-and-a-half years old, deal with her dad re-entering her life after an absence of one year or so? We split up shortly after she was born and he had some contact limited to odd visits after that, before he moved away for work. Now he is back in the country and wants to resume contact with her. She seems to be having some difficulty in comprehending it all and I would like to help her make the transition in the best way possible for her sake.

A. Restarting contact between a parent and child after a gap can be a delicate matter and you are right to think carefully as to how to go about it. It is common for there to be a break in contact immediately after separation as it is a natural instinct when a relationship breaks up for ex-partners to want to move away from one another and start a new life elsewhere. However, this is not compatible with co-parenting, which requires that both parents continue to negotiate and work with one another for the sake of the children. Making this transition to co-parenting while living separately can be hard, but over time it does become easier.

NEGOTIATE WITH HER FATHER

Generally, the single biggest factor in determining how children cope after their parents separate is the level of co-operation between said parents. Try to agree a co-parenting plan in advance of the contact starting. If this is hard, seek the help of a family mediator who can help you start to communicate and work out this important agreement.

EXPLAIN IT TO YOUR DAUGHTER

It is understandable that your daughter might be unsettled by what is happening. As she has not had consistent contact with her father since she was an infant, and given that there has been a gap of a year, she does not have an established relationship with him. She is likely to be confused about his role in her life and possibly nervous about restarting contact.

Try to explain the situation to her in a way that she can understand. For example, you might create a little photo album that has pictures of all the people in her family. This can include pictures of her father – one of when you were together as a couple and one of him more recently. Tell her a simple story (appropriate to her age) of how Mammy and Daddy met, how they decided to live apart, how Daddy went to live away and now he is back in the country.

Remember, how she feels about starting contact will be largely determined by the feelings you communicate about it. If you are upbeat and positive about this new start, this will help her feel the same way. You should also try to manage her expectations, as she might have great hopes about what this contact could mean (sometimes children have a fantasy that their parents will get back together again). Be clear and matter-of-fact about the reality of your relationship with her father.

START GRADUALLY AND GO AT YOUR DAUGHTER'S PACE

The key to restarting contact is to do so gradually and to go at your daughter's pace. The first step might be her father sending her a card, a picture and some information, followed by visits to his home where she will see him with you present. The next step might be a visit from him in your own home, during which you give them space. A later step can be him taking his daughter out. Try to facilitate and support her relationship with her father by setting things up well for them both.

BE AWARE OF YOUR OWN FEELINGS ABOUT THE SEPARATION

Be aware that restarting contact could bring up old hurts and resentments for both you and your ex-partner. Indeed, many parents can be angry when the other parent makes contact after a gap, as they have been coping alone for many years and the change can be quite disruptive to their lives. Be aware of how you are feeling so you can put these feelings in context and focus on the needs of your daughter.

Do consider contacting support services to help you. I would also encourage her father to seek support, as it can be particularly challenging to be in the position of trying to restart contact with his daughter.

My son's father won't stay in contact with him and he is really upset

Q. *I split up with son's father four years ago, when our son was three years old. His father did keep intermittent contact but this has waned over the years. Particularly now, he seems to have less time for his son as he has just had a new baby with a new partner and lives a bit further away. This is very hurtful to my son, who has more or less said to me that he thinks his dad loves the new baby more. His father even missed his birthday party last week (though he did come with a gift the next day). I have tried to talk to his father about it and he just says he is busy with family and work and says he will get back to me. To be honest, I feel really angry with him. I also think his new partner is putting pressure on him and is trying to stop him spending time with our son. I know it is none of my business, but she seems very controlling. I am just worried about my son who idolises his dad. I also know how important it is for fathers to stay involved, especially for boys, and I don't want my son to miss out. What can I do?*

A. Unfortunately, your situation is not uncommon. When parents separate, frequently contact with the parent who leaves the family home can reduce significantly over the years. As you have discovered, this reduced involvement often happens when the live-away parent remarries or has more children, or if they move to a new area. Though in modern times the situation is getting better, it still remains a challenge to ensure both parents maintain a quality relationship with their children post-separation. As a mother you are commended for being so aware of the importance of your son's relationship with his father and for making efforts for this to be maintained.

NEGOTIATE WITH HIS FATHER ABOUT CONTACT

While it is important to be understanding of the pressures on his father with a new baby and living further away, it is important to assertively request that he makes a commitment about contact with his son. Be careful about blaming anyone, such as his partner, for the lack of contact as this may be unhelpful (ideally you need her support for contact to go well), and instead focus on negotiating the contact your son needs. When contact is unpredictable it can be upsetting for children, and for this reason it is important to agree on a basic weekly routine that works for everyone.

Write to his father and explain how important a contact routine is, and ask him to phone or meet you to agree on this. When you talk, explain how much his son idolises and needs him and how upset he is when contact does not happen as expected. Try to present this in a non-blaming way. Try to make a written co-parenting agreement that you both commit to. You could seek the help of a family mediator to assist you in making this plan.

LISTENING TO YOUR SON

Take time to listen and help your son express his feelings and wishes. When he feels let down by his father, don't add to his upset by saying how angry you are too; instead, try to help him have a balanced understanding of his father's actions, for example: 'It is a pity that your dad couldn't come to the party, but it is good that he can come tomorrow.' Be reassuring if your son expresses concerns about his father loving the new baby more: 'I don't think that is true – you know how much he loves you – it is just that new babies take up a lot of time.'

HELPING YOUR SON TALK TO HIS FATHER

It is also useful to help your son communicate his feelings directly to his father. In my experience, children are often afraid to communicate unhappiness to the parent who lives way from the home, fearing that they will pull away more. As a result, it is often the parent who looks after them most of the time who gets the brunt of the child's anger and upset.

It would be great if your son's father could listen to his feelings. The important thing is for his father not to respond defensively, and instead to listen and be reassuring about how much he loves him. You could facilitate this conversation by arranging that the three of you sit down and talk together about how contact is going and by encouraging your son to share how he feels. Have a chat with his father before doing this so he can be prepared.

FOCUS ON WHAT YOU CAN DO

You cannot make his father increase or regularise his contact. While you can be positive and support your ex-partner's involvement, at the end of the day there is only so much you can do and it is primarily his father's responsibility to prioritise his relationship with his son. You also have the important role of supporting your son whatever relationship he has with his father, and of helping him manage this the best way he can.

My ex-girlfriend doesn't want me to have anything to do with my ten-month-old daughter

Q. *I am a separated father and my daughter is ten months old. My ex-girlfriend discovered she was pregnant shortly after our relationship ended. Since my daughter has been born, things have been difficult with my ex and she only allows me to see her for about one or two hours each week. I am hoping to increase this and to be more involved in my daughter's life, but my ex says she does not want this and last week threatened to cut off all contact. In return, I threatened to take it to court. What legal rights do I have? We weren't married but I lived with my ex for two years.*

A. As an unmarried father you have no automatic legal rights and depending on where you live you may have to apply to the court to gain guardianship or parental responsibility. There is good information on this process and on the challenges of being an unmarried father on www.treoir.ie (Ireland), www.lawandparents.co.uk (UK). However, the best way to be more involved in your daughter's life is by agreement with her mother. While, of course, you have a right to go to court and you should get the best legal advice, there are many dangers associated with a legal process – it can increase the antagonism with your daughter's mother and this does not serve you in having a better relationship with your daughter. Therefore, the first port of call is to try to come to an agreement about shared parenting with your daughter's mother. The better you can communicate and work civilly with your ex as co-parents, the easier it will be to have a good ongoing relationship with your daughter.

WORKING WITH YOUR DAUGHTER'S MOTHER

Take time to understand your ex's point of view and where she might be coming from. Is there a particular reason that she does not want to increase the contact? Perhaps she is reluctant to share the care of her daughter for a longer period or perhaps she finds the practicality of the contact difficult to accommodate. Perhaps she is still upset about the break-up and finds contact with you difficult. The more you can understand where she is coming from emotionally, the easier it will be to negotiate with her.

Focus on your daughter's needs and try to persuade her mother of the value of your ongoing involvement as a loving father. Try to make any increased contact you have fit in with her schedule. For example, offer to mind your daughter when she is working, busy or needs a break, or agree to allow a third party, such as a grandparent, to manage the handover if that is easier.

You should also make sure to share in all the parental responsibilities of caring for a baby (financial, practical and emotional), so that your daughter's mother sees you both as a resource to her daughter as well as to her as co-parent. Show her, in words and deeds, that you are committed to parenting your daughter and to supporting her as your daughter's mother.

Finally, if it is difficult to have these conversations, contact a family mediation service and seek their assistance in negotiating a solution, or attend a parenting-when-separated course or a support group for fathers.

My three-year-old daughter is reluctant to come into contact with me

Q. I *separated from my wife two years ago, when my daughter was fourteen months old. It was a difficult time with a lot of conflict and I did not see my daughter for a few months. About four months ago, I got back into regular contact with my daughter through the courts and I have access twice a week. The problem is that my daughter is often reluctant to come with me and my ex-wife tells me she is anxious about the contact and upset when she comes back. I am not sure whether to believe my ex who just wants me out of her life. What can I do?*

A. In the context of conflictual separation it is a challenge for the parent who leaves the home (usually the father) to maintain contact with children, especially when they are very young. Your situation is made harder by the fact that there was a long gap of no contact with your daughter, meaning that you are effectively at the stage of trying to re-establish a relationship with her. Given that she is so young, and primarily attached to her mother, she may well be anxious about the contact and unsettled by this.

FIND A WAY OF GETTING THE SUPPORT OF HER MOTHER

The key to moving forward is to try and get the co-operation of your daughter's mother. The more she can be positive and reassuring about your role in your daughter's life, the easier your daughter will settle. When her mother raises concerns, ask her for advice and assistance in helping your daughter settle and enjoy contact with you. Can you change how contact and visits are organised to make your daughter more comfortable? Could you spend some time playing with her in her home (with her own toys, etc.) and with the clear support of her mother? Or could the three of you visit a playground together and let your daughter see her mother's support on the trip? The more your daughter sees the two of you communicating civilly and normally, the easier it will be to have contact. Alternatively, you could visit another family member that she knows well during contact (such as a grandparent) or take her to an activity she is familiar with, as this might put her at ease.

If it is hard to negotiate with her mother about contact, do consider getting some help and going to family mediation or some other support services.

My six-year-old son doesn't want to see his dad

Q. *I recently separated from my husband and have been in the family law court five times trying to sort out access arrangements for our six-year-old son. The court granted an interim protection order against his father due to excessive alcohol consumption mixed with antidepressants – his behaviour was very distressing to both our son and myself. Following a psychologist's report, he was granted day access with supervised handover and return. He used only two of these visits, then stopped, saying I was the problem and that he would wait until his son could decide for himself about contact. He has not seen his son since late last year and now he wants to make contact again. Our son previously found access distressing – he had nightmares, slept badly and was very anxious until visits stopped. Now he is sleeping through the night and his self-esteem and confidence are soaring. When I ask him if he wants to see his father, he says, 'No thanks, can't you see I'm happy now?' I've also always offered him the possibility of phoning his father, but he never has. Family law states it is beneficial for a child to see both parents. Have any studies been carried out to show that one-parent families can work and that when a parent's behaviour is negative that the child is better off without that parent until they sort themselves out?*

A. Family law is right to hold the ideal that it is beneficial for a child to have contact with both parents and for both parents to make a contribution to a child's life – in general the research studies back this position up. The exception is when this contact leads to serious conflict and stress for the child or when one parent is behaving very negatively (for example, alcohol and drugs), which can mean they are unable to care for the child.

However, even though you and your son have had negative experiences in the past, it is important to hold open the possibility that his father may have moved on and that he may be able to have a constructive involvement in his life (either now or at some point in the future). It is important to remember that parenting is a long-term project. A caring father involved in his son's life is important not just now, but when your son hits his teens, and even beyond, when he becomes a young adult. It is also important to note that while, on average, children do better with two caring involved parents, many single parents can happily bring up children. Though it can be much harder parenting alone, many parents compensate for this by gaining extra support through extended family and friends.

PARENTS NEED TO DECIDE WHAT CONTACT ARRANGEMENTS ARE BEST

Each child and each family situation is different, so you must decide on what is best for your son. I do think that your son is too young to make this decision himself. He is likely to mainly remember negative experiences about his father, which are colouring his perception. The thought of contact may conjure up a fear of returning to previous conflicts and upsetting experiences, and he may not as yet be able to imagine a positive way of his father being involved while you are separated. Furthermore, at six years of age, children from separated families frequently experience a divided sense of loyalty and feel they have to make a choice of one parent over the other – but this choice is a terrible burden to them as they grow up. While, of course, you will listen to him, it is important that he understands that it is your decision (along with his father and the court) about what the contact arrangement is. This should be a relief to him and take the burden of having to decide away.

EXPLORING HOW CONTACT MIGHT HAPPEN WITH HIS FATHER

If his father is currently asking for contact, it is worth exploring ways of this happening in a positive way. This might, of course, require very careful planning and arrangement. If possible, you should first talk this through with his father and, if need be, seek a third party to help you negotiate an arrangement, such as a professional mediator or family counsellor. The key to making this work is for the two of you to move towards a more civil relationship with each other and to reach an agreement about contact centred on your child's interests – this is a tall order, but it might be possible over time.

Because of your son's distress about access in the past, this new contact may need to start gradually. This might begin with his father writing a letter to your son, explaining his feelings and his wish to be in contact. The more positive he can be the better. The contact can build up gradually, leading to his father phoning regularly and making short visits. To make this work it is crucial for you to be supportive, to talk positively about contact and do all you can to facilitate this. It is also essential for his father to take the initiative, to keep any promises he makes about contact and to be prepared to go at his son's pace and accept his feelings.

You and his father may need some assistance, either together or separately, from a professional such as a family counsellor to make these steps.

HELPING YOUR SON HAVE A BALANCED UNDERSTANDING OF HIS FATHER'S PAST

Whatever the level of contact, it will help your son to have a balanced understanding of his father as he grows up. Even if your former husband has a problem with alcohol or drugs, it is important to help your son know another side to his father and for him to have a sensitive awareness of previous difficulties according to his age and level of understanding.

STEP-PARENTING AND NEW RELATIONSHIPS

My daughter won't accept discipline from my new partner

Q. *I was a single mother for many years and then I met a new partner four years ago. I have a thirteen-year-old daughter who was nine when she first met my partner. My partner has always been wonderful to my daughter and they get on great as a rule. However, she does not accept discipline from him and this causes lots of conflict, particularly since she became a teen. Do you have any guidance on how I should manage this?*

A. Introducing a new partner to your children and creating a new family unit is a complex process at the best of times. Everyone is faced with the challenge of working out new relationships. Your partner must deal with the challenge of forming a relationship with your daughter and working out how much of a stepfather role he should adopt. You are faced with the challenge of moving from being a single parent to including your partner in the family and balancing your relationship with both of them.

UNDERSTANDING DIFFERENT ROLES AND RELATIONSHIPS IN BLENDED FAMILIES

While things can often go very well, there can be conflict, particularly if you have different expectations of each of the relationships and how people should fit in. For example, whereas you may expect that your partner would be able to adopt a stepfather role in your daughter's life, this may not be the way she sees things. She might see your partner as just that and not expect him to be a father to her.

Your daughter was relatively old when your partner was introduced to her and though she might see him as supportive or even a fun person in her life, she might not expect him to adopt a parental role, particularly when it comes to discipline. In addition, although she might get on with him most of the time, she might also feel rivalry towards him – after all she had you to herself for nine years and now she has to share your attention.

Though you don't mention any details, another factor is whether your daughter has or has had a relationship with her birth dad, her perception of him and the circumstances in which you became a single parent.

DEALING WITH ISSUES WITH A YOUNG TEENAGER

All these issues can come to a head when children hit the teenage years. At thirteen it is very normal for children to begin to separate and pull away from their parents. They begin to question their parents' rules and start a journey towards independence and making their own decisions.

As parents you can experience this as conflict because your rules and values are challenged, and it can feel a bit like a rebellion. Questions about identity and belonging are very significant during the teenage years and your daughter may be wondering about her birth father and her origins, as well as rethinking her relationship with you and questioning the role of your partner. Setting rules with teenagers can be a challenge in most families and you have the extra challenge about her identity to consider. To resolve things, I would make a number of suggestions.

HAVE REALISTIC EXPECTATIONS ABOUT ROLES

First, it is worth rethinking and examining your own expectations. If your partner has not had a disciplinarian role up until now, then it might be unrealistic for him to adopt this as your daughter becomes a teenager. Generally in blended families it is okay for you, as the birth parent, to be the main disciplinarian and for your partner to be in a support role.

You should insist that your daughter displays respect to your partner (and vice versa), but making decisions about rules and boundaries is mainly your responsibility. You should also chat through these issues with your partner and explore what his expectations are. It may be a relief to him that he does not have to be the main disciplinarian, and that he can mainly focus on being a supportive person towards you and your daughter.

TALK THINGS THROUGH WITH YOUR DAUGHTER

Second, it is worth sitting down and trying to talk to your daughter about the issues. Ask how she is feeling about things in the family at the moment and directly raise the issue about how she sees your partner and his role in the family. Then you can share your hopes and expectations (for example, that you hope that they will continue to get on and that you expect her to be respectful and not rude towards him). At an appropriate time, bring up a conversation about her birth father. Check how she is feeling about this and whether she wants any more information about the past or even if she wants to make contact at some point in the future. The more you can be open and listen to her, the better for her in the long term.

ATTEND TO YOUR RELATIONSHIP WITH YOUR DAUGHTER

Third, as much as possible try to keep your relationship with your daughter positive. Make sure you have one-to-one time with her during the day, when you chat and enjoy each other's company. Though this can be harder when children become teenagers, it is just as important – the more you maintain a connection, the easier it will be to resolve discipline issues.

Notice what interests you have in common, what things you enjoy doing together and when you have the best chats, and make sure to build on these. Equally, it is important for your partner to continue to cultivate his relationship with your daughter, while taking into account that she is now a teenager and may be questioning his role in the family.

How can I be a good stepmother to a six-year-old boy?

Q. *I am due to get married soon and my partner has a six-year-old son from a previous relationship. The plan is for him to live with his mother half the week and with us the other half of the week. I feel very daunted at the prospect of becoming a stepmother and I am aware of everything that can go wrong. Do you have any tips on making it go well?*

A. When you get married to someone who is a parent, you are not only taking on a new relationship with them, you are also committing to a significant relationship as a step-parent to their children. Just as being married involves negotiating the sometimes tricky relationships with in-laws and your partner's family, you also have to take into account the relationship with your partner's six-year-old son's mother (and possibly her family) as well.

THE CHALLENGE OF BECOMING A STEPMOTHER

While there are plenty of issues for men becoming stepfathers, there are particular challenges for women becoming stepmothers as there can be such expectation and intensity about the mothering role. Mothers are expected to take on the central caring role, especially when children are young, and this can lead to jealousy and competition between mothers and stepmothers. Your stepson's mother could feel threatened if you take on too much of a central caring role and, equally, could be critical of the quality of your parenting if you take no active role.

CREATING A HAPPY BLENDED FAMILY

Creating a comfortable and happy blended arrangement can often take time and patience, and there is no one-size-fits-all approach as each family is different. A lot depends on how each of you (your partner, your stepson, his mother and yourself) feel about the new arrangement and, in particular, what expectations you all bring about everyone's respective roles and relationships.

YOUR PARTNER'S COMMUNICATION WITH HIS SON'S MOTHER

You don't give many details in your question, but how does your partner get on with his ex? If they had a good co-parenting relationship prior to your arrival, and she is happy enough with him getting married (so they can move on with their lives), then this is something positive to build upon. If their relationship is more problematic or hostile, that does make things more difficult and it is important for your partner to do what he can to improve things in order to constructively co-parent with his son's mother.

This means that your partner should communicate directly with his ex about the issues affecting his son and work hard at reaching an agreement about parenting arrangements. However, remember this negotiation role is his and not yours. While you should encourage him to work towards achieving a civil relationship with his ex, it is generally not a good idea for you to get directly involved.

YOUR RELATIONSHIP WITH YOUR STEPSON

How things will work out depends a lot on how you currently get on with your soon-to-be stepson and how he feels about his father getting married. Give him lots of space and time to adjust and be sensitive to how he feels and thinks. He may fear that your arrival will mean he will lose quality time with his father or that it will affect his relationship with this mother. He needs to be reassured that you are not a threat to either of these relationships, and that your arrival means the gain of a new attentive adult in his life, rather than a loss of someone.

One of the key issues for children whose parents are separated is managing a divided sense of loyalty. They can feel caught in the middle of their parents' original dispute and can feel they have to choose or take the side of one parent over the other. This is particularly the case if the relationship between his parents is not amicable. It is possible that he might feel that accepting your role as stepmum is a betrayal of his mother, especially if he senses she is unhappy about the arrangement. If this is the case, it really helps if you and your partner are sensitive to his feelings and relieve him of having to choose.

Finding words to explain to him what is happening in a positive way is crucial. For example, you might take time to acknowledge how important his mum is and how much he loves her, as well as explaining that you want to get to know him and to care for him too. If possible, you can point out that he now has a stepmum as well as a mum who loves and cares for him.

YOUR PARTNER'S RELATIONSHIP WITH HIS SON

In developing your relationship with your new stepson, it is important to go slowly and at his pace, and to be wary of rushing or jumping in to 'being mum'. It is probably best that his father remains in the main parenting role in terms of care and discipline and that you only slowly take on these roles.

Certainly, it is important that his father prioritises special time with his son and regularly checks in with him about how he is feeling and what he is thinking. You should make sure to talk through all these issues with your partner and to listen to his concerns and expectations too. The more you can find a shared understanding and learn to support each other in your new roles, the better for everyone.

For many children, the inclusion of a new step-parent in their life is a good thing, as it brings a new person into their world who is interested and attentive to them. This is particularly the case if all the adults in the family are happy about what is happening. If a child senses that his father is happier because of the marriage and that his mother is at least okay about it too, then this will help him accept and even enjoy the new arrangement.

My boyfriend wants me to meet his five-year-old daughter. Is it too soon?

Q. *My boyfriend of eight months has a five-year-old daughter from a previous relationship. He separated from his ex eighteen months ago and sees his daughter a few times a week. Our relationship is going well and the question has come up about meeting his daughter. He has her for a full six days at the end of the month and he was wondering if we could all go away somewhere together for part of this. I feel a bit nervous about meeting her and am wondering if there is any advice or tips you can give on making it go well. There is also the problem of how her mother might react. My boyfriend's relationship with her can be difficult and she has never really accepted them splitting up. Sometimes she threatens to reduce his contact. I don't know how she will react when she discovers he is going out with someone new.*

A. Moving on and starting a new relationship post-separation can be a challenge for everyone involved. Frequently, for young children, a parent's new relationship can bring up the hurt of the original separation and end the fantasy that their parents might get back together again. Furthermore, when one parent starts a new relationship, children can experience a divided sense of loyalty, especially if the other parent has not moved on and is unhappy with this new development. For example, if a boy forms a friendship with his father's new girlfriend, he can feel he is somehow being disloyal to his mother. He can also feel worried and insecure that the arrival of a new partner in his father's life might reduce his own importance.

GOING SLOWLY AT YOUR PARTNER'S DAUGHTER'S PACE

The key to helping children in this position is going slowly and being very sensitive to their feelings. Generally, the advice is not to introduce a child to a new partner for some time, until you are sure that the relationship is a long-term feature of your life. It also helps to think carefully about how you introduce a child to a new partner and to make sure that they are ready. It is good that you and your boyfriend are taking time to think all this through.

I'm not sure if going away together on holiday is the best way to start this introduction, as this might be too much too soon. Generally, the best way is to start gradually, maybe for a short time initially and then building up slowly. Perhaps, during the six days, her father could make a plan for the two of them to meet up with you a few times over the period.

YOUR PARTNER SHOULD TALK THINGS THROUGH WITH HIS DAUGHTER

Before meeting you, it is also important that her father sits down and talks through the situation with her, explaining that you are a new person in his life whom he hopes she will get to like. He should clearly indicate that your arrival does not change her relationship with him, or her relationship with her mother.

He should have this conversation alone with her, so she is free to share her feelings with him. He should be prepared to talk to her a few times about it. Often when you give children important news, they need time to process it before they are aware how they feel or can think up their questions. There are some useful story books that positively explain forming new families that he could read with her, such as *It's Not Your Fault, Koko Bear* by Vicki Lansky.

COMMUNICATING WITH HIS DAUGHTER'S MOTHER

Before meeting you, it would also help if her father could communicate directly with her mother about his new relationship with you. My advice to separated parents is that if they are going to introduce a new partner to a child, they should be prepared to communicate this to the other parent first. This saves the child from feeling they know a secret, worrying what the other parent might think, or witnessing the other parent's reaction when they find out. This is, of course, a difficult communication to get right, although it can be best done in a concise, matter-of-fact way: 'I am just letting you know that our daughter will be meeting my girlfriend this weekend.' The introduction of a new partner could put tension on their co-parenting relationship, especially if she has not moved on from the original separation. Your boyfriend should anticipate this and work hard to positively communicate and seek mediation if necessary.

MEETING HIS DAUGHTER FOR THE FIRST TIME

When you do meet your boyfriend's daughter for the first time, it should be low-key and informal – perhaps the three of you could go for a short walk. In forming your relationship with her over time, the key is to go slowly and not to expect too much. You should make sure that she continues to get alone time with her father and that she does not see your presence as a threat to this.

Take your time in getting to know her, focusing on establishing a friendship with her. Don't expect to be adopting a parenting or disciplinarian role in the near future – that is her father's place. Also, it is very important that you speak positively about her mother in front of her and are sensitive and supportive about her relationship with her.

Finally, although being introduced to and getting on with a new partner's children can be a delicate process, in many situations it can go very well. Lots of children I work with accept their parent's new relationship, especially if they see that it makes their parent happier and it does not compromise their own relationship. They can also gain a new supportive person in their life and, handled well, this can be a bonus to them.

Introducing a new partner to a toddler

Q. *I have a question about introducing a new partner to a toddler as a separated father. Basically my daughter is almost three years old and I'm wondering how best to manage the introduction of a new partner in her life. My daughter typically sleeps over with me on a Saturday night and I would like us both to be able to stay at my new partner's house rather than my own.*

A. If your relationship is steady and going well with your partner then it may be time to introduce your daughter to them. The general principle is to go slowly. It is a big step to take your daughter on a sleepover to your partner's house, where she will be in an unfamiliar setting. It might be better to start more gradually, maybe with your partner meeting your daughter at your house when your daughter is staying, then building up to your partner staying over in your house when your daughter is there, before taking the step of all of you staying in your partner's house.

GO SLOWLY AND NOTICE HOW YOUR DAUGHTER RESPONDS TO EACH STEP

The key is to tune into your daughter and to notice how she is responding to each step. Hopefully she will get on with your partner, which will make things a lot easier, but if she does not, you need to take a step back and to consider how best to approach things. Either way, she will probably need to be reassured that the inclusion of your partner in her life does not reduce her importance in your eyes. She will need to see that you still spend quality time with her.

COMMUNICATE WITH YOUR DAUGHTER'S MOTHER

It is also important to communicate with your daughter's mother about what is happening. Though this is a delicate conversation to get right, if done well it can free up your daughter from thinking your new partner is a secret not to be told to her mother. This will help her feel more relaxed with your new partner.

SINGLE PARENTING

Meeting new partners as a single parent

Q. *I read your answer recently about the right way and time to introduce a new partner into a child's life, and it has led to renewed discussion about this issue with friends of mine who are also single mothers. We all agree with the approach of taking it slow, but we feel a need for some new ideas, especially for single mums who do not have a lot of support with their children, and who are simply not free to meet with a new partner over an extended period of time before introducing him. How do you do this when your child is almost always with you? How do you get to the stage where you are sure 'a new partner is a long-term feature' when you can only carve out a meeting here and there, after the child is in bed and all involved are bone-tired, if no one takes your child overnight or for a day at the weekend? Of course, you can introduce a man as 'just another friend', but experience shows that children sense the difference. Also, some children seem to have a desire for a new partner or a man in their life and are eager to attach. Any ideas? I would be interested in your advice because if you search the internet for advice, it mainly says wait until you are sure you're going to marry the new man, but this is unrealistic in many circumstances.*

A. Your question raises a number of challenges for separated and lone parents when it comes to trying to meet new partners and make new relationships work. Even when parenting with a partner, raising children can be time-consuming and stressful and there can be little time to attend to the couple's relationship. The situation is harder for many separated and lone parents who are doing the lion's share of parenting and there can be even less time for personal projects or new relationships.

GAINING SUPPORT AS A LONE PARENT

There is an old proverb that says 'it takes a village to raise a child', meaning that to really parent a child well, you need many supportive people in their life. The lone parents I know who cope best create links with other people and draw in close friends and family to help them. This might mean that you rely more on grandparents, aunts, uncles or other lone parents who can share some of the tasks of parenting with you. It is also a reason to try to re-engage the children's father to get him to share more in the parenting. Even if this was not possible in the past, this does not mean that you might not be able to reach out and involve him more now.

MAKE SURE A NEW RELATIONSHIP IS STEADY BEFORE INTRODUCING THE CHILD

You are right that the most important principle in forming a new relationship as a parent is to go slow and to ensure it is steady before introducing the person to your children. This is not only because the children might be unhappy with the new relationship but also, as you rightly say, because they may attach to your partner quickly and be devastated if the relationship ends.

In dating and getting to know potential partners, I think you have to try to be creative to find ways of meeting them without necessarily involving your children. Could you and the other single parents form a babysitting rota that supports each of you in turn going on dates? Or are there other family members who you could rely on? Even if you aren't interested in dating, it is a good idea to try to include other people to help you care for your children, so you get time to pursue personal projects and your children have contact with other supportive adults.

As a separated father, how can I make their second house a homely one?

Q. *My wife and I separated recently. There was no one else involved. We have two girls aged eight and six. Both are happy where they live with an extensive network of friends. For practical reasons it was decided that I would move out of the family home. I have established myself in a new location about ten minutes' drive from the family home. My ex and I have decided that the children should stay with me on Wednesday and Saturday nights. While I have been reasonably successful in establishing a routine on Wednesdays, most of the time the girls end up back at the family home on Saturdays playing with their friends. I am receiving conflicting advice as to how I should proceed. On the one hand, I'm told that if you establish a firm and fixed routine, the girls will adapt. On the other, I'm told to take it slowly and allow the girls to find their own rhythm. If I don't, then my children could end up resenting staying in the new location. My ex is of one mind and I am of the other in this regard. I have always been heavily involved in the rearing of our children and am frustrated and anxious about the future. However, I would be willing to follow either path if it's good for the children.*

A. Generally, the parent who leaves the family home post-separation can be at a disadvantage when it comes to maintaining contact and being actively involved in their children's lives. Moving out can mean that you have less time with your children, and you have the extra challenge of establishing a new home, both for you and your children.

FEELING SECURE POST-SEPARATION

As you have discovered, children tend to have an attachment to the original family home and to their established networks of school, local friends and amenities. This attachment to their 'home' can become important post-separation, as they have been through many changes and they often feel secure by keeping some things the same in their lives. Establishing a new home for your children in a different locale can take time and patience. Initially, the new home can be uninviting, and children can miss their familiar friends, toys and routines. In these situations, it is easy to feel rejected as a parent and you may be tempted to back off. However, it is important to realise that your girls need a quality relationship with you more than ever post-separation and you have to work harder as the non-residential parent to stay involved.

BEING FIRM OR GOING AT YOUR GIRLS' PACE

You are receiving conflicting advice that you should either go at their pace and respect their natural gravitation back to the family home or that you should put your foot down and insist they spend Saturday nights with you. I think the truth lies somewhere in the middle and you have to take into account both principles. I think you need to understand that they need some stability in their lives and that doing some of the usual things on a Saturday night is helpful for them, but equally you need to begin to establish a new routine with them post-separation that matches the long term.

ESTABLISHING NEW ROUTINES IN YOUR HOME

It would help if you could think of their perspective and try to understand what would make the Saturday more appealing for them in your new home (making sure they have some of their belongings with them, considering inviting over familiar friends and family, etc.). Simple things like involving them in the choice of furniture in their bedrooms or doing a family decorating project can make a difference. You need to start new interesting routines with them in your new home, such as cooking together or going for a walk in a local park.

At six and eight, your girls are at a good age to talk through options. Sit down with them and listen to their ideas and feelings. Things seem to be going well on the Wednesday night. Think about what works in the routine that night. Could you consider a second weekday night as an alternative?

AGREE A WAY FORWARD WITH THEIR MOTHER

The key to moving forward is negotiating an agreed solution with your girls' mother. Children generally toe the line if both parents decide on an agreement. If you are in dispute, try to seek mediation in order to reach a resolution. The important thing is to focus on your children's needs, which includes a quality relationship with both their parents. You must co-operate and co-parent constructively and understand your girls' need for security (and thus minimise changes post-separation).

CONSIDER CREATIVE SOLUTIONS

There are a number of creative solutions that you can bring to the table. For example, you could agree with your children's mother that you will spend Saturday and Sunday in the family home with the girls while she goes out or spends time elsewhere. This can work well for an initial transition period as you establish your new home and a good routine for the children. Some modern thinking about parental separation proposes that the original family home should be seen as the children's home rather than belonging to the parents, and that the parents can take alternate times being responsible for the children in this house. This can break a common post-separation scenario where you might have a residential parent who is burdened by the challenges of parenting largely alone and a non-residential parent who is struggling to stay involved.

Single parent feeling guilty

Q. *I'm a single mum to a three-year-old boy. I'm also a mature student in college and lately I have noticed my son's behaviour has changed and I'm wondering what the problem may be and what I can do to try to alleviate it. He is very outgoing and socially able but lately he is acting like a teenager and gets very cross and upset if he doesn't get his own way. While I'm sure this is normal to some degree and he is only asserting himself, I feel his behaviour goes beyond this and I'm wondering is this something he is learning from me. He has a great relationship with his dad, whom he stays over with two nights a week, and his dad adores him but does not discipline him. He often calls in and, when both of us are there, he condones bad behaviour while I'm trying to correct it. I think our son sees this and perhaps both of us are wrong. I don't know how to communicate with our three year old that he cannot scream and get cross constantly.*

I'm under pressure in my final year of college and perhaps he is picking up on this. He goes to a crèche for half the week and the staff say he is getting on great there and they have not noticed any changes. I suppose my real worry is that I'm somehow causing all this. I try not to show my stress in front of him but perhaps I'm not doing a great job. We spend lots of quality time together and do lots of activities. However, recently he has stopped wanting to do these things. Is this telling me something?

A. Whatever the specific causes, screaming when angry and displaying tantrums are relatively normal behaviours for three-year-old children. When faced with this behaviour, it is easy as a parent to react by correcting, criticising and battling with children to behave, especially when you feel stressed or under pressure. However, such reactions can inadvertently reinforce your child's misbehaviour and all too easily become a habit between the two of you that can wear both of you out and damage your relationship.

TAKING A 'PAUSE' TO DEAL WITH TANTRUMS

If you find yourself constantly correcting your son, or always on his case to behave, or if you feel you are regularly in a battle with him, then it is important to take a step back and to try to find more positive ways to manage. In dealing with his tantrums, the key is to make sure you are able to pause and to not get hooked into reacting emotionally to his negative feelings. Then it is important to respond thoughtfully and calmly with a range of strategies that can include asking him to express himself rather than screaming ('use your words to talk to Mum') or by soothing him ('I know you are upset, let's calm down now') or by distracting him ('Let's go and play with the toys') or giving him a choice ('You can have the toys when you ask politely'), etc. Occasionally, you may have to take some action, such as putting him somewhere safe to calm down for a moment or physically taking a step back yourself to do something else and put space between you.

FOCUSING ON YOUR SELF-CARE AS A PARENT

Responding positively and thoughtfully as a parent is hard work, particularly if you are stressed and managing without support. In addition, feeling guilty or blaming yourself does not help you or your child and can increase the pressure on you unnecessarily. The most important thing is to be compassionate towards yourself as a parent and to take practical steps to reduce the stress in your life. Simple changes, like reorganising routines, prioritising relaxation time and learning positive discipline techniques, can make a big difference.

FOCUS ON DOING FUN, ENJOYABLE THINGS WITH YOUR SON

It can be more valuable if you can incorporate fun and time for chatting with your son into everyday chores, such as getting dressed in the morning, or having breakfast or even tidying up in the evening. This would really reduce the stress within the day and help him co-operate more.

CO-PARENTING WITH HIS FATHER

The fact that his father and you manage your son's behaviour differently may not necessarily be a significant factor. In my experience, children can tolerate a great degree of difference between parenting styles when their parents are separated, as long as the two parents support one another and it is clear which parent is in charge at a given time. Also, when visiting your home, it is possible that his father defers to you to manage your son's behaviour and this is not an indication as to how he might discipline his son in his own home when he is in charge.

However, as co-parents it is a good idea that you work together to support one another and, if possible, you should sit down with his father and talk through the issues and come up with a shared plan. Most importantly, your focus should be on establishing your own confidence as a parent in your home, and achieving a balance between supporting and enjoying your son as well as correcting and disciplining. If you are interested in finding out more, consider attending a parenting course where you can learn more positive discipline ideas in a supportive group atmosphere.

Dreading Christmas as a separated father

Q. *My wife and myself separated last February. We had not been getting on for several years and I finally moved out and now live with my father. I thought things might improve with us living apart, but in fact they seem to have got worse and it has been very hard the past year for me to see my two boys, aged four and six. Through the court, I have been granted weekend access and once during the week. This has been going okay, though my boys are reluctant to stay over with me at their grandfather's house. Because they live nearby, they often prefer to go home and sleep in their own beds. Over Christmas, the court ruled that I can see my children on Stephen's Day and the New Year, but they will stay with my ex-wife for Christmas Eve and all of Christmas Day. As we come to Christmas I realise how much I am going to miss them this year. I feel I have been treated unfairly and am cut out of a lot of their lives. To be honest, I feel in a much worse position than I was last Christmas. Even though there was a frosty silence between my wife and me, at least I was there with my kids. Now I will be alone.*

A. Experiencing relationship breakdown and separation is one of the hardest things you can go through as a parent. It is particularly challenging at Christmas when family events and togetherness are highlighted and your own particular losses are experienced acutely. The first Christmas is often the hardest, when you are adjusting to a new living situation that might be still far from ideal. As a father, not being there with your children for the special moments of Christmas Eve and Christmas morning can be very hard and this can be especially difficult if you are alone yourself. Though it can seem like a workable practical arrangement for one parent to have the children at Christmas and the other at the New Year, frequently this is difficult for the children and the parents who might prefer more frequent contact at this special time of year.

NEGOTIATE WITH THEIR MOTHER ABOUT CHRISTMAS ARRANGEMENTS
While it may be short notice to try to change this year's arrangements, there may be some scope for negotiating with their mother about making things a little easier. Perhaps there is scope for you to visit on Christmas

morning or to take them out for a short walk, or perhaps you can at least talk to them on the phone or by Skype on Christmas morning. How much you can negotiate depends, of course, on the relationship you might have with their mother.

In trying to reach an agreement, it is very important to try to see the situation from her point of view as this will help you reach better compromises. For example, though you might think she is coping well, it is quite likely that she will be experiencing her own acute upset and loss at Christmas. As the residential parent she is probably dealing with the challenges of parenting and the demands of the two children alone and without the support she would like. The more you can avoid blame and try to understand things from her perspective, the easier it will be to negotiate better solutions.

UNDERSTAND THINGS FROM YOUR CHILDREN'S PERSPECTIVE

It is also helpful to consider how your children might be feeling this Christmas. Generally, young children find their parents' separation stressful and frequently get caught up in their parents' conflicts and can feel emotionally stuck in the middle. They value it enormously if both their parents remain involved in their lives and if they learn to get on and co-parent appropriately.

They can find it harder to stay connected with the parent who has left the family home and can need support regarding this. Wanting to return home to their own beds is completely normal and represents their need for things to be secure and the same in changing times. Try not to feel rejected by their behaviour and patiently persist in staying involved and building a second home for them.

MAKE THE MOST OF THE ARRANGEMENTS YOU HAVE

Even if it is not possible to change things this Christmas, commit to making things the best they can be for your children and yourself. Make a plan for how you might use the time you have with the two children. Try to think of rituals, events or visits you can do with them that you might all enjoy and that will be meaningful to you.

Make a plan also for the time you will be alone and be sensitive to your own feelings of upset at Christmas. Post-separation, parents' own mental well-being can take a nosedive, so try to be aware of this. Avoid negative coping strategies such as drinking and instead reach out and get some support. The better you're coping personally, the better you can parent your children.

TAKE A LONG-TERM PERSPECTIVE

In the aftermath of a separation, relationships between parents can be challenging as ex-partners try to work out new living arrangements, which might be more difficult for both of them in the short term. However, with time and perspective things can improve and it is important to hold on to this. Make a plan to seek support next year to resolve things better for yourself and your children.

SPECIAL PROBLEMS

Should I take my ten-year-old son to counselling to help him deal with the separation?

Q. *My partner and I have gone our separate ways. I would like to bring our ten-year-old son to talk things out with a counsellor. Is this a service you provide or do you know who does?*

A. I would think carefully before taking your child to a counsellor. While some children can benefit from counselling when their parents are separated, for some it can be unhelpful. This is especially the case if they are not ready to talk about their experiences or if they interpret going to counselling as indicating that they are somehow at fault for their parents' difficulties.

CONSIDER A GROUP PROGRAMME FOR YOUR CHILD
Participating in a group programme, where the focus is on helping children cope, can sometimes be more beneficial for them, and they meet other children from separated families and gain the message that they are not alone. Some of these are run in schools and community centres such as the Rainbows courses (www.rainbowsireland.com) or other groups are run in therapeutic centres, such as the Daughters of Charity Family Resource centres (www.docchildandfamily.ie). Counselling can often be beneficial to older children and teenagers, who can make their own decision to attend facilities such as the Teen Between service (www.teenbetween.ie).

MAKE SURE TO MANAGE THE SEPARATION WELL AS PARENTS
However, what really helps children cope with separation is how their parents manage it. There are a lot of very positive things you can do to help your son, such as keeping conflict with your partner to a minimum and making a decision to positively co-parent together. In addition, it is important to listen to your son's individual needs, and in the face of the

stress of separation make sure to maintain the quality of your parenting. It can really help to minimise disruptive changes for your child, such as moving school, location or losing contact with grandparents or special friends. The more you support your son's contact with friends, family and leisure pursuits that matter to him, the better.

It is important to remember that coming to terms with your parents' separation is a long-term process, so it is important to periodically check in with your son to see how he is doing. Make sure to ask him at different times about the changes he has experienced. Be prepared to listen to his feelings and to accept any upset or anger about the separation in a non-defensive way. While at some point counselling might help, being able to communicate with you will help him the most in the long term.

My ex-husband has a strong dependence on alcohol

Q. *My ex-husband had, and still has, a strong dependence on alcohol. We live separately and generally have a good working relationship. But occasionally the children's father phones and, under the influence of drink, says out-of-hand things. How do I help my children (aged fifteen and thirteen) deal with this, as the incident may not be acknowledged again yet can upset them, particularly my fifteen-year-old son, who is striving to have a relationship with his dad?*

A. At the best of times, discussing alcohol dependency with a family member is a delicate issue. Depending on how they view their alcohol consumption or their behaviour under the influence, there is always the danger that they will react defensively and, if their denial is strong, may even pull away from you as the person who challenged them.

Things are all the more delicate when you are separated and more work needs to be put in to maintain relationships. You want to deal with the issue in a way that actually helps your children's relationship with their father and in a way that does not damage your good working relationship with him (which is a real asset when parenting together as a separated couple).

DISCUSSING THE ISSUE WITH YOUR CHILDREN

If the children were younger, it would be your responsibility to raise the subject with their father and take steps to ensure that he is not under the influence when in contact with them. As they are older, it is also appropriate to involve them in the conversation about what happened and to first explore with them their ideas about how best to deal with the situation.

The first thing to do is to ask your children how they feel about what happened. Have they told you directly about what their father said and how they feel about it, or have you inferred what happened and that they were upset? If you have not done so already, pick a good time to talk to your children individually about what happened. For example, you could talk to your son when you have a bit of time together.

Depending how sensitive an issue it is, it can help to raise the subject gently by, for example, asking him: 'How did you feel about the conversation with your father on the phone the other night?' Then, depending on how he responds, you could probe a little bit further and raise the drinking directly: 'Your father sounded funny on the phone *and/or* he made some out-of-hand remarks – I think he might have been drinking.' The key is to give your son space and to listen to his response.

It is also important not be judgemental about their father, but rather be factual about what happened. If appropriate, you can express an opinion – 'I wish he wouldn't call when he is drinking' – but it is also important to ask what your son thinks, as he has to begin to work out his own relationship with his father.

EXPLORE HOW YOUR SON WANTS TO COMMUNICATE WITH HIS FATHER

Explore with your son what he wants to do about what happened. Does he want to say something to his father about it (which might be a big ask) or would he like you to mention something to his father (you might discuss what you would say together), or would he prefer to leave it and not say anything for the moment? You should listen carefully and try to take your son's views into account. Depending on how the conversation goes, it could provide an opportunity to discuss a range of issues, such as the effects of drinking in general, his father's alcohol dependency in particular – and even the past and your separation. These are very delicate conversations to get right.

HELPING YOUR SON UNDERSTAND

When parents separate, children tend to feel caught in the middle and can easily feel a divided sense of loyalty and a pressure to take sides. It really helps if you can talk about what happened in a way that frees your son from having to take the side of one parent or the other. Try to explain the issues about his father's drinking in a sympathetic way that enables him to understand his father better, but also in a way that gives him clear information and lets him make up his own mind about his father's problem with alcohol. Generally, teenagers value it if you tell them in an adult way why and how the separation has happened. Remember that teenagers can appreciate that there are two sides to the story, and it can be very helpful to explain to them your views and feelings, and then to objectively and fairly describe the other parent's views as well. This can relieve them of the burden of having to take sides and help them maintain a connection with both parents.

DISCUSSING THE ISSUE WITH THEIR FATHER

Depending on how serious the issue is, how frequently it happens, and whether it is blocking your children's relationship with their father, it may be appropriate to raise the incident directly with their father yourself. In doing this, it can really help to try to pick a good time to talk and then to be as matter-of-fact as possible, saying, for example: 'When you rang the other night, you seemed to have had a few drinks. The children noticed because you made a few off-hand remarks that upset them. I'd appreciate if you could not drink when you are making contact.' It can help to emphasise the positives, such as: 'The children really value your contact and I appreciate that we have a good co-parenting relationship.'

SEEKING SUPPORT

Remember, there are also other sources of support both for you and your children such as Al-Anon, which is a self-help group for relatives affected by a family member's drinking, and specifically Alateen, which is for young people dealing with these issues (www.al-anon-ireland.org). There is also a national drink and drug advisory helpline 1800-459459, as well as www.drugs.ie, which has lists of local family services for anyone affected by problematic drinking.

My ex was violent towards me before we split up and I'm worried about him having contact with our son

Q. *I left a very unhappy marriage just under a year ago. My husband was a drinker and he could be aggressive and violent. I left with my son, now five, after one big episode of violence that my son witnessed, and went to live with my mother. His father has not been in touch much since then, except for two times when he called to my mother's house. When he became verbally aggressive my mother threatened to call the police. It was a very stressful and difficult time but my son and I are finally getting back on our feet. Since I left I have been feeling much better and I realise how much he intimidated me throughout our marriage, and though there was only sporadic violence, I was completely controlled by him. Luckily I was renting with my ex-husband, so living separately has been less complicated financially.*

Recently, I received a solicitor's letter saying that my ex-husband was seeking shared custody and contact with our son and I am not sure what to do. I know he is his father, but I worry about his drinking and violence. I also dread the thought of having anything to do with him, but will do it if it's best for my son.

A. Violence in the home leaves a terrible legacy for everyone concerned and the first priority should be safety. It is good that you had the courage to act and to move to a safer place when you had to. As you indicate, the dynamics of intimidation and control that underpin violence and the threat of violence can be particularly damaging. Breaking the silence, acknowledging what is going on and seeking support are all important steps in moving forward.

CHILDREN HAVING CONTACT WITH A PARENT WHO HAS BEEN VIOLENT
In incidences of domestic violence, what ongoing relationship the parent should have with their children is a complicated question. A simple ban on contact is not necessarily in the children's interest, as this removes the possibility of healing and a good relationship with their parent in the future. Also, such a ban can leave a lot of issues unresolved for children

and they can build an unhelpful fantasy about the parent they don't meet. Furthermore, they can interpret the fact that their father is excluded as meaning that there is something wrong with them too (as they share 50 per cent of the genetics). Such fantasies can be grounded by some ongoing, ordinary contact with the parent. On the other hand, simply agreeing to extensive contact with a parent who has been violent without addressing the issues of violence and ensuring safety can be harmful if it means the intimidation and violence is continued.

WHAT ROLE YOUR SON'S FATHER SHOULD HAVE

What role your son's father should have in his life now depends on a number of factors. It centres on how much he is willing to take responsibility for the violence in the past and how ready he is to be involved and take on a positive role as a father. The ideal is that his father is willing to seek help for his drinking and to manage his violence, and is prepared to move on constructively. The fact that he has now made contact via his solicitor should be seen as an opportunity to assess the above and to restart constructive contact if it is possible. For example, you could reply to his solicitor's letter (via your own solicitor) saying that you would welcome a constructive role for your son's father, but you would need to be assured that the violence and drinking problems have been addressed first. You would also need the contact to start gradually and in a supervised way to ensure everyone is safe. You could also ask for an initial stage of mediation to happen or for his father to attend specialist counselling before anything is agreed.

SEEK SPECIALIST ADVICE AND SUPPORT

In your situation, I would suggest you seek specialist legal advice and support before responding to his letter (see a list of organisations at the end of this book). It is likely to be difficult to deal directly with your son's father so do get support around this. There are some specialist family counselling agencies that could help you. Some of these agencies (e.g. Relationships Ireland) might be able to help you mediate with your son's father. For example, they might meet you first and then invite his father into the process so that you can make an agreement about what is best for your son. A skilled therapist should ensure that the issues of violence are kept to the fore and correctly dealt with, and that safety is what is prioritised. Additionally, your solicitor and legal services should be able to advise you on your range of options moving forward.

My ex-wife is aggressive and I'm worried about my daughter

Q. *I split from my wife just over a year ago. Despite being married for ten years it had been a very unhappy marriage. My wife would constantly belittle me, and could be very aggressive and volatile towards me. Things went badly wrong after my daughter (now six) was born – my wife found parenting hard and was depressed and unhappy. She took things out on me and insisted I leave the bedroom (I have learnt subsequently that she was unfaithful to me on a number of occasions). I finally left when I met someone through work who has shown me what a real, loving relationship is like. Though she had no interest in me, my wife did not take the break-up well, and became really aggressive. When I tried to talk to her she hit me and destroyed some of my possessions. On one occasion, in a rage, she lifted a knife and threatened to kill me.*

When I moved out, I continued to be involved as a father and my daughter stayed over with me several nights a week. However, my wife has done everything she can to disrupt this. Last year she made an accusation to child protection services that I had harmed my daughter – this devastated me and it meant that I did not see my daughter for six weeks while this was being investigated. Of course, there was no substance to it and the social workers privately shared to me their worries about my wife's mental health. Since that time, contact with my daughter has been difficult and my wife can be volatile. I am increasingly worried about her mental health (she is drinking heavily) and her ability to care for my daughter, though she refuses any increased contact or involvement from me (I am happy for my daughter to come and live with me full-time). It seems very difficult to get legal support to change things and I know that if I take a court case my wife will be livid and may take it out on me and stop contact altogether. I also know that the court could decide against me. What do you advise?

A. Sadly it is not uncommon for parents to make unfounded accusations of child abuse within the context of serious acrimony. Unfortunately, in my work as a social worker I received very many of these referrals. Sometimes the parent making the accusation would be deliberately using this as a means to attack the other parent or to stop them having contact with their child. More frequently, they were so upset, angry and mistrustful of the other parent that they strongly believed the child should only live with them and that the child was at risk of harm with the other parent. Whatever the reasons, such allegations represented deep acrimony and resulted in a breakdown of communication between the two parents.

SEEK SPECIALIST SUPPORT AND ADVICE

In the situation that you are dealing with it is important that you seek specialist support and advice. As a first port of call you may wish to re-contact the social workers that were involved in the investigation. Explain to them your concerns for your daughter and ask for their assistance. They could reassess the situation and refer you and your ex-wife to specialist therapeutic services. For example, it may be helpful to seek the support of a skilled family therapist or mediator who could work with you and your wife to reach an agreement focused on your daughter's needs. They also have recourse to legal options as necessary to protect your daughter.

In addition, you should seek your own legal advice about your options. In your situation it may be helpful to get a court order that formally recommends the best custody and access arrangements for your daughter. While there is a danger that starting court proceedings may antagonise your ex-wife, particularly in the short term, you may need to do this for the sake of your daughter in the long term. A wise court judgment has the potential to support an arrangement that is in your daughter's best interests (e.g. shared custody with you as residential parent) and from this position you can negotiate more easily with your ex-wife. The court also has recourse to recommending specialist family assessments that may be beneficial for deciding what is best.

SEEK SPECIALIST SUPPORT AS A NON-RESIDENTIAL FATHER

Seeking court judgments can, of course, be risky, and frequently the judgment leaves one parent (or even both) unhappy, or the court process itself is too crude an instrument to focus on the needs of an individual child. Court judgments are often biased against fathers, especially non-residential fathers. Courts can be reluctant to countenance judgments against mothers or to conceive that a mother's parenting could be sub-standard and that children may be better off living with their fathers. For these reasons, be cautious and realistic about what you hope for. Seek support from specialist groups for fathers in similar situations to your own.

BEHAVE POSITIVELY TOWARDS YOUR WIFE

After all that has happened, it would be understandable if you were extremely angry with your ex-wife. Do not let this affect your judgement or willingness to collaborate with her. Remember she is, and always will be, the mother of your daughter and it is in your daughter's interests for you to work as co-parents the best way you can. Even if your ex-wife has behaved irrationally, don't be tempted to do the same in return. It can be helpful to be understanding of the upset that might underpin your wife's actions. As you said, she may be deeply unhappy and struggling with mental health and alcohol problems, and may need some help and support to overcome these problems. Her long-term well-being is important to your daughter and thus important to you as her father. At all stages in the process, be open to negotiation and making agreements with your daughter's mother where possible. Do make the most of the contact you currently have with your daughter and try to build on this.

FOCUS ON YOUR DAUGHTER'S NEEDS AND WHAT IS BEST FOR HER

Don't lose sight of what is best for your daughter. Try to set goals based on her needs and work towards these. Is it best for your daughter to live with you, with her mother maintaining contact? Or is the idea of shared custody and a shared parenting arrangement more suitable? How can you and her mother move to the point where you can work together as co-parents for the sake of your daughter? Be prepared to be flexible, creative and persistent for the sake of your daughter.

USEFUL RESOURCES

Parenting Courses

PARENTS PLUS: PARENTING WHEN SEPARATED PROGRAMME

In order to address the challenges of parenting when separated, Parents Plus have developed a six-week psycho-educational course for parents who are preparing for, going through or have gone through a separation or divorce. The Parenting When Separated Programme aims to help parents:

» Solve co-parenting problems in a positive way that focuses on the needs of children;
» Cope with the emotional impact of separation and learn stress management techniques;
» Help their children cope with the impact of the separation both emotionally and practically;
» Enhance communication with their children and with their children's other parent.

Website: www.parentsplus.ie/separation

Legal Advice and Mediation Services

AIM FAMILY SERVICES

Family law information, family mediation and counselling centre.
64 Dame Street, Dublin 2
Tel: (01) 6708363 (Monday to Friday, 10 a.m.–1 p.m.)
Email: aimfamilyservices@eircom.net
Website: www.aimfamilyservices.ie

FAMILY MEDIATION SERVICE

The State provides a free family mediation service nationally for couples who have decided to separate or divorce and who want to negotiate on the terms of their separation, and addresses issues such as living arrangements, parenting and financial issues. See the Legal Aid Board website for a list of services.

Tel: (01) 6725886

Website: www.legalaidboard.ie

FLAC (FREE LEGAL ADVICE CENTRES)

Provides free legal information and a referral telephone service where you can get the details of your nearest centre.

13 Lower Dorset Street, Dublin 1

Tel: (01) 8745690

Information and Referral Line: 1890 350250

Website: www.flac.ie

Note: Ask for solicitors who provide collaborative law services, which has the emphasis on helping couples resolve legal matters co-operatively and in a non-adversarial manner.

LEGAL AID BOARD

Offers free legal advice on matters of civil law to those who do not have the resources to fund such services.

Head Office: Quay Street, Cahirciveen, Co. Kerry

Tel: (066) 9471000/1890 615200

Dublin Office: 47 Upper Mount Street, Dublin 2

Tel: (01) 6441900

Email: info@legalaidboard.ie

Website: www.legalaidboard.ie

Support Services for Parents

Separation can be a stressful and emotional time for many people. You can be left with feelings of anger, hurt and guilt. It can be hard to know where to turn or how to best help you and your children through this difficult time. However, there are many services available that can provide counselling, parenting support and advice.

ACCORD

Offers support for couples and individuals in their marriages and relationships.
Central Office, Columba Centre, Maynooth, Co. Kildare
Tel: (01) 5053112
Email: info@accord.ie
Website: www.accord.ie

ALCOHOLICS ANONYMOUS

Offers support groups for those struggling with alcohol addiction.
General Service Office of Alcoholics Anonymous,
Unit 2, Block C, Santry Business Park, Swords Road, Dublin 9
Tel: (01) 8420700
Email: gso@alcoholicsanonymous.ie
Website: www.alcoholicsanonymous.ie

AL-ANON IRELAND

A support service offered to families and friends dealing with the effects of living with an alcoholic family member or friend.
Al-anon Information Centre, 5 Capel Street, Dublin 1
Tel: (01) 8732699
Email: info@al-anon-ireland.org
Website: www.al-anon-ireland.org

AMEN

Support for males experiencing abuse in an intimate relationship.

St Anne's Resource Centre, Railway Street, Navan, Co. Meath

Tel: (046) 9023718

Email: info@amen.ie

Website: www.amen.ie

AWARE

Services for people affected by depression, including a confidential phoneline service.

National Office, 72 Lower Leeson Street, Dublin 2

Tel: (01) 6617211

Email: info@aware.ie

Website: www.aware.ie

HSE (HEALTH SERVICE EXECUTIVE)

Offers a range of free services to those experiencing mental health difficulties, including anxiety, depression, psychosis, etc. Services include Primary Care Psychology and Community Mental Health Services. Should you be concerned about your mental health, please contact your GP for information and referral to services in your area.

Website: www.hse.ie

MABS (MONEY ADVICE BUDGETING SERVICE)

Free financial advice.

Helpline: 0761 072000 (available Monday to Friday, 9 a.m.–8 p.m.)

Email: helpline@mabs.ie

Website: www.mabs.ie

MOVE (MEN OVERCOMING VIOLENCE)

Facilitates groups for violent men who hope to overcome their difficulties.
Unit 2, First Floor, Clare Road Business Mall, Clare Road, Ennis, Co. Clare
Tel: (065) 6848689
Email: move@moveireland.ie
Website: www.moveireland.ie

ONE FAMILY

Services and support for one-parent families, including training, education
and a confidential helpline.
Cherish House, 2 Lower Pembroke Street, Dublin 2
Tel: 1890 662212/(01) 6629212
Email: info@onefamily.ie
Website: www.onefamily.ie

PARENTLINE

Confidential helpline for parents under stress or who are worried about
any aspect of parenting.
Carmichael House, North Brunswick Street, Dublin 7
Tel: (01) 8733500/1890 927277
Email: info@parentline.ie
Website: www.parentline.ie

RELATIONSHIPS IRELAND

Offers a wide range of services to address relationship issues, including
couples counselling, separation counselling (which is offered on a one-to-
one or couples basis), co-parenting consultations to resolve co-parenting
difficulties, Life After Separation and Divorce workshops and separation
support groups.
38 Upper Fitzwilliam Street, Dublin 2
Tel: 1890 380380
Email: info@relationshipsireland.com
Website: www.relationshipsireland.com

ROLLERCOASTER
Provides practical advice on the challenges facing parents. Chat forums are also available.
Website: www.rollercoaster.ie

SAMARITANS
Confidential helpline and support for people in distress.
4–5 Usher's Court, Usher's Quay, Dublin 8
Tel: 116 123 (24hrs)
Email: jo@samaritans.org
Website: www.samaritans.ie

SOLO
Supports people parenting alone through the provision of a wide range of information, including family law, child education and monetary matters.
Email: info@solo.ie
Website: www.solo.ie

TREOIR
Provides free information and referral services regarding pregnancy, counselling, social welfare and legal rights.
14 Gandon House, Lower Mayor Street, IFSC, Dublin 1
Tel: 1890 252084
Email: info@treoir.ie
Website: www.treoir.ie

UNMARRIED AND SEPARATED FAMILIES IRELAND
Support for separated fathers, mothers and grandparents.
Website: www.uspi.ie

WOMEN'S AID
Support for women who are experiencing abuse in an intimate relationship.
Open 10 a.m.–10 p.m. seven days a week, except Christmas Day.
5 Wilton Place, Dublin 2
Helpline: 1800 341900
General Enquiries: (01) 6788858
Email: info@womensaid.ie

Support Services for Children Experiencing Parental Separation
Children can experience a range of emotional reactions to parental
separation, and for some it can be difficult to talk with their parents. There
are a number of supports available to children who are struggling to adjust
to their new family situation. Should you have serious concerns in relation to
your child's behaviour or social or emotional adjustment, please discuss this
with your GP, who may have additional knowledge of local services available.

BARNARDOS
Has a wide range of services working with children, families and
communities.
National Children's Resource Centre, Christchurch Square, Dublin 8.
Tel: (01) 4549699
Email: info@barnardos.ie
Website: www.barnardos.ie

CARI
Provides a confidential helpline and other services for those with concerns
in relation to child sexual abuse. The helpline can also be used to receive
information or advice on other issues relating to children.
110 Lower Drumcondra Road, Dublin 9
Lo-call helpline: 1890 924567
Email: helpline@cari.ie
Website: www.cari.ie

CHILDLINE

A confidential listening service for children up to the age of eighteen. The website provides information on a range of issues such as separation and bullying.
Freephone helpline: 1800 666666
Text support: Text 'talk' to 50101
Website: www.childline.ie

CHILDREN'S RIGHTS ALLIANCE

Provides information on developments affecting children in Ireland under the UN Convention on the Rights of the Child.
31 Molesworth Street, Dublin 2
Tel: (01) 6629400
Email: info@childrensrights.ie
Website: www.childrensrights.ie

HEADSTRONG

Works with communities in Ireland to support the mental health of young people aged between twelve and twenty-five.
Website: www.headstrong.ie

HSE (HEALTH SERVICE EXECUTIVE)

Offers a range of free services to children experiencing emotional or behavioural difficulties including Primary Care Psychology Services, Community Child and Family Services and Child and Adolescent Mental Health Services. In order to access services, referrals are usually sent by GPs. For information on the appropriate HSE service in your area, please contact your GP.
Website: www.hse.ie

RAINBOWS

Facilitates groups to help children, teenagers, young adults and parents who have experienced loss through death, separation or divorce.

Rainbows National Office, Loreto Centre, Crumlin Road, Dublin 12

Tel: (01) 4734175

Email: ask@rainbowsireland.com

Website: www.rainbowsireland.com

TEEN BETWEEN

Counselling service, run by Relationships Ireland, to help children between twelve and eighteen years to cope with their parents' separation or divorce.

38 Upper Fitzwilliam Street, Dublin 2

Tel: 1800 303191

Email: teenbetween@relationshipsireland.com

READING MATERIAL

For Parents

Hall, P., *How to Have a Healthy Divorce* (Relate, 2008).

— *Help your Children Cope with Your Divorce: How to Lessen the Pain of Divorce for your Children* (Relate, 2007).

Hayman, S., *Moving On: Breaking Up Without Breaking Down* (Relate, 2001).

— *Step Families: Living Successfully With Other People's Children* (Relate, 2001).

Litvinoff, S., *Starting Again: How to Learn From the Past for a Better Future* (Relate, 2001).

McGhee, C., *Parenting Apart: How Separated and Divorced Parents can Raise Happy and Secure Children* (London: Penguin, 2010).

— *Separate Yet Successful: Restructuring Family Life After Parents Part*, http://www.divorceandchildren.com/parents.html.

O'Hara, L., *When a Relationship Ends: Surviving the Emotional Rollercoaster of Separation* (Dublin: Blackhall Publishing, 2011).

Quilliam, S., *Stop Arguing, Start Talking: The 10-Point Plan For Couples in Conflict* (Relate, 2001).

Sharry, J., *Positive Parenting: Bringing Up Responsible, Well-Behaved and Happy Children* (Dublin: Veritas, 2008).

— *Parenting Teenagers: A Guide to Solving Problems, Building Relationships and Creating Harmony in the Family* (Dublin: Veritas, 2013).

Sharry, J., Hampson, G. and Fanning, M., *Parenting Preschoolers and Young Children* (Dublin: Veritas, 2005).

For Children

Good, G., *When Parents Split: Support, Information and Encouragement for Teenagers* (Dublin: Blackhall Publishing, 2008).

Gray, K., *The Mum and Dad Glue* (London: Hodder, 2009).

Heegaard, M., *When Mom and Dad Separate: Children Can Learn to Cope with Grief* (Minneapolis: Woodland Press, 1991).

Lansky, V., *It's Not Your Fault, Koko Bear: A Read Together Book for Parents and Young Children Going through Divorce* (Minnesota: Book Peddlers, 1998).

Masurel, C., *Two Homes* (London: Walker Books, 2002).

McGhee, C., *Lemons 2 Lemonade*, http://www.divorceandchildren.com/parents. html.

Thomas, S. and Rankin, D., *Divorced But Still My Parents: A Helping Book About Divorce for Children and Parents* (Dublin: Springboard Publications, 1998).

For Group Leaders and Professionals

Brosnan, E., Beattie, D., Fitzpatrick, C. and Sharry, J., *Working Things Out 2: An Evidence-Based Mental Health Resource For Professionals Working With Young People in Clinical and Community Settings* (Dublin: Parents Plus, 2011), www. parentsplus.ie.

Sharry, J. and Fitzpatrick, C., *Parents Plus Adolescents Progamme: A DVD-Based Parenting Course on Managing Conflict and Getting on Better with Older Children and Teenagers Aged 11–16 Years* (Dublin: Parents Plus, 2009), www. parentsplus.ie.

Sharry, J. and Fitzpatrick, C., *Parents Plus Children's Programme: A Video-Based Parenting Guide to Managing Behaviour Problems and Promoting Learning and Confidence in Children Aged 6–11* (Dublin: Parents Plus, 2008), www. parentsplus.ie.

Sharry, J., Hampson, G. and Fanning, M., *Parents Plus Early Years Programme: A DVD-Based Parenting Course on Promoting Development and Managing Behaviour Problems in Young Children Aged 1–6* (Dublin: Parents Plus, 2009), www.parentsplus.ie.

Sharry, J., Madden, B. and Darmody, M., *Becoming a Solution-Focused Detective: Identifying Your Clients' Strengths in Practical Brief Therapy* (London: Routledge, 2011).

Sharry, J., Murphy, M. and Keating, A., *Parents Plus: Parenting When Separated Programme* (Dublin: Parents Plus, 2013), www.parentsplus.ie.

Sharry, J., *Counselling Children, Adolescents and Families: A Strengths-Based Collaborative Approach* (London: Sage, 2004).

Sharry, J., *Solution Focused Groupwork* (London: Sage, 2008).

For further parenting articles and features, please visit John Sharry's website: www.solutiontalk.ie.